Thank God It's Monday!

A Tool Kit for Aligning Your Lifevision and Your Work

By
Tim Hoerr

Nashville, Tennessee
Copyright © 1998

Published by Everywhere Press
1501 County Hospital Road
Nashville, Tennessee 37218

Printed in the United States of America
ISBN 1-58029-101-5

Library of Congress Cataloging-in-Publication Data:
Hoerr, Tim
Thank God It's Monday : a tool kit for aligning your lifevision and
your work / Tim Hoerr.
p.   cm.
ISBN 1-58029-101-5
1. Conduct of life. 2. Life change events--Religious aspects.
3. Goal (Psychology) I. Title.
BF637.C5H64 1998   98-18435
158.6--dc21   CIP

To my loving wife, Toni.
Your love and encouragement have
made our lifevision journey a profound joy.

Contents

Part I
Discovering Your Lifevision

Part II
Aligning Your Lifevision and Your Work

Part II
Renewing Your Lifevision

"Employees are working too hard, too long, with too little appreciation. Companies are starting to look very seriously at this issue of career-life balance, but there haven't been enough creative programs to address it."

—Bonnie Bachman, "CareerDirections,"
Chicago Tribune, Dec. 28, 1997

"If we all worked on the assumption that what is accepted as true is really true, there would be little hope of advance."

—The Wright Brothers

Introduction

Everywhere these days, I hear a common refrain that goes something like this:

"Oh, it's Monday. Ugh."

"Tuesday. A little better, but ugh, wish it were Friday."

"Hump day — a good sign — yes, we're going over the hump."

"A muffled 'hooray' — it's Thursday — we're almost there."

"THANK GOD IT'S FRIDAY! The weekend has arrived. Now I can really live."

Sound familiar? It's become a cultural norm, a cliché of everyday existence. Many of us are living for the weekend and work only because we have to. Life happens on the weekends, doesn't it?

Something is seriously wrong here. We're looking to the weekend and thanking God it's Friday so we can really live, so we can do something meaningful, restful, or refreshing. But in fact, the very thing we're seeking — to live life to the fullest — may be getting farther out of reach. We have failed to see the subtle deception at the center of this modern cultural phenomenon. We've bought into the paradigm of TGIF and haven't noticed the bum rap we got as a result.

We need a mind shift, a brain realignment — we need a new paradigm! We need the paradigm of "Thank God it's Monday!"— a new way to find meaning and satisfaction as much on Tuesday as Saturday. We need to find fulfillment in our work by discovering our purpose and aligning our work with it. We need to continually renew ourselves to that purpose, so that we're charged with energy at the start of the week as well as at its conclusion. I'm recommending that we adopt a new way of living, relating, and working. I'm talking about **lifevision** — a fresh, practical look at the topic of personal purpose.

I recognize that countless books have been written on the topics of personal effectiveness and success. In fact, the commitment to a personal purpose is usually included as one of a list of six, eight, or ten ingredients essential to achieving personal success. So, you might ask, " Where does the discovery and alignment of personal purpose rank in the overall scheme of things?" This is a very important question, and few people have taken the time to examine the answer.

I believe the discovery, alignment, and renewal of your personal purpose are the foundations of achieving personal effectiveness and success. Their importance is usually diminished, however, by inclusion in a list of seven habits, ten principles, or eight keys to successful living. We read these lists and measure ourselves against them, and yet most of us don't spend enough time really exploring our purpose. We are much too casual about it; we move on to the other items on the list too quickly. This is a big mistake. I hope that the presentation of some timeless truths about personal purpose — in the format of lifevision — will help you understand this vital topic in a new way.

I hope that wrestling with your lifevision proves to be one of the most meaningful things you'll ever do. If done with care and thoughtful contemplation, it can have a profound impact and perhaps radically alter your future. Lifevision deserves its own concentrated study separate from the other elements for achieving success. Wrestling with the tough questions and digging deep for honest answers requires your undivided attention. This book is a collection of tools and ideas to help you in that process.

Once you begin the journey of discovery, you'll find that it is a lifelong process, always evolving and never ending. In some sense, you never "arrive." But I want to encourage you to start the journey, and assist you along the way.

Unlike so many business books, this one is not just for business executives and leaders. While leaders will find it very useful, it is just as much intended for the "everyday worker." The stories I share in the book are from the entire spectrum of the workplace. Most of the stories are about ordinary people who, like you are seeking meaning and purpose in their work.

Lifevision: A Fresh Look at Personal Purpose

Lifevision comprises three key elements:

- Purpose (WHAT) — both your present understanding of your personal purpose and the picture of your preferable future
- People (WHO) — the relationships through which you live out your personal purpose
- Principles (HOW) — the guidelines by which you fulfill your personal purpose

Many treatments of the topic of personal purpose stop with the first element of lifevision: Purpose. Yet the other two elements (People and Principles) are just as vital to understanding and living out your personal purpose. The process is similar to an painting a portrait. To define your "mission in life" only in the context of Purpose (the first lifevision element) is to paint a flat, one dimensional picture. The People and Principles elements add texture and a three dimensional nature to the artwork, bringing it new meaning and vibrancy. What I will do in this book is take you on the journey of exploring each of the three foundations of life-vision.

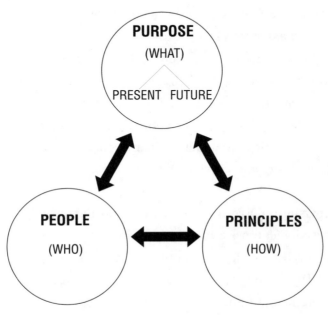

As you discover and mold your lifevision, it will become a powerful tool, guiding you on the exciting journey of life. The process will allow you to feel truly empowered and energized as you move forward. Even in the most difficult of times, your life-vision can act as the point of reference to guide you through. Most importantly, a lifevision can propel you toward the fulfill-ment of your unique destiny. There can be no greater satisfaction than this in life!

Lifevision in Three-Part Harmony

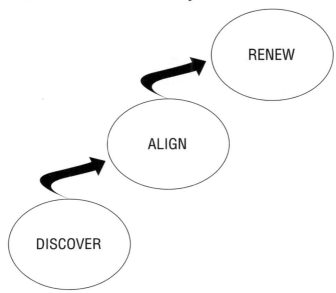

The book is arranged in three parts. Part One deals with the discovery process, and it is indeed a process. I'll present a framework for the initial and ongoing discovery of your lifevision by devoting a chapter to each of its three main elements: purpose, people and principles.

Part Two deals with aligning your lifevision with your work. Because you spend the vast majority of your waking hours involved in some type of work, you should actively pursue the alignment of your lifevision with your work.

Part Three addresses the challenge of renewing your lifevision, day in and day out. As we will all face plenty of difficulties in fulfilling our lifevision, we need some tools to keep our vision fresh and to solidify our commitment.

At the end of each chapter are tool kit exercises to assist you in applying the lifevision concepts. Although it's easier to skip the exercises, I encourage you to take the time to work through them. The discovery and alignment of lifevision isn't easy. It will take determination and hard work on your part, but I think you'll find the results will be worth the effort.

Life is both a journey and a destination, and that is a paradox. It was Einstein who said that the closer you get to truth, the more it appears to be a paradox. That should not stop your pursuit, however! Reading this book is just one way you can make a little more sense of the paradox in your life. I trust that it will help you discover meaning and purpose in your life, Monday through Sunday. Welcome aboard for the ride!

I invite you to send me your lifevision stories by mail, fax or e-mail. If you have a story or illustration about your lifevision or the lifevision of someone you know, I encourage you to send it to me. I would enjoy hearing about successes and failures alike! In particular, if you have a work situation where you have found great alignment and real personal satisfaction, I want to know about it.

Tim Hoerr
McGladrey & Pullen, LLP
3111 Camino del Rio North, Suite 1150
San Diego, CA 92108
(619) 280-3022
(619) 280-6902 (fax)
tim_hoerr@rsmi.com

Part I
Discovering Your Lifevision

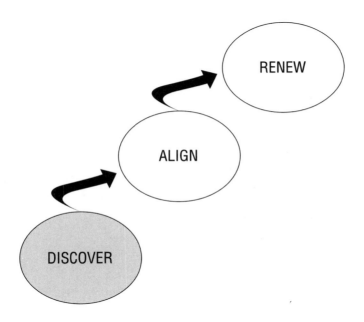

Chapter 1

Framework for Discovering Purpose

*"Everyone has his own specific vocation or mission in life
to carry out a concrete assignment which demands
fulfillment. Therein he cannot be replaced, nor can
his life be repeated. Thus, everyone's task is as unique
as is his specific opportunity to implement it."*
—Viktor E. Frankl,
Man's Search for Meaning

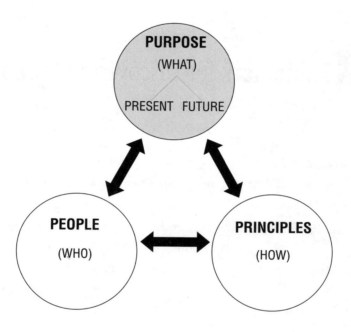

There's a story told of an individual who wanted to take a Caribbean cruise. Ever since he was a little boy he dreamed of being on a fancy cruise ship, sailing into exotic ports of call. Unfortunately, he found himself constantly frustrated by lack of funds. He needed to discipline himself to set aside the money for the trip. One day he decided to do just that. He would save $50 a month until he had enough to afford the lowest cost cruise available.

After a couple of years of scrimping and pinching, the big day arrived. With incredible excitement, he boarded the cruise ship. For two weeks he enjoyed the sights, sounds and smells of cruising the Caribbean. This was living! Yet there was a peculiar note of sadness to the whole adventure. Having paid only the bargain fare, each night he watched the evening celebration and dinner from a distance. He ate the fruit and sandwiches he had packed for himself, but what he really wanted was something — anything — from the lavish smorgasbord. The food selections were astounding. The choicest prime rib, the freshest seafood, the tastiest accompaniments, the finest wine and desserts. On top of it all, everyone seemed to be having an extraordinary time. Each evening was full of laughter and conversation, dancing and fun. He was desperate to enjoy the festivities. If only he had been able to save enough money to afford something more than the bargain cruise!

On the last evening of his vacation, one of the ship's stewards spotted the man watching the dinner celebration from a distance. And the celebration that night was awesome! The music rocked the night air. The food selection was more extravagant than ever. The passengers were having the time of their lives. It was toward the end of the evening that the steward finally approached the man and asked, "Why aren't you joining the grand finale cele-bration?"

"For the same reason I skipped all the other evening festivi-ties — I only purchased the lowest cost excursion," the man replied. A look of sadness crept across the man's face.

"What?! All the cruise fares, no matter the price, include all evening celebrations — unlimited dining, dancing and festivi-ties," declared the steward.

The man was dumbstruck. The horrible realization took just a few moments to sink in. What a mistake he'd made! For two weeks he had eaten apples, oranges and sandwiches for dinner — watching other guests eat, drink, and celebrate in style. He sim-ply hadn't thought to ask, and now it was too late. How could he have made such a mistake?

He was disgusted — mainly with himself. Where had his head been? For three years he had saved his money for the trip of a lifetime, only to miss out on one of the cruise's central features! The food and festivities had been included all along. The pain of the squandered opportunity was great, and he would live with the regret forever.

Like the man on the cruise ship, you're on the journey of life. And there are some important questions you need to ask yourself, questions that will make a significant difference in how you expe-rience the journey:

"What's included on the trip?"
"What's my life all about?"
"Is there a meaning and a purpose to my existence?"
"How can I maximize my life's journey?"

Surprisingly, many of you are not asking these questions, nor are you taking the time to find the answers. I know because I've talked with many of you. The day-to-day activities and commotion of life keep you occupied. There is precious little time to stop and reflect on life's most important questions. But if you're not asking the questions and seeking the answers, what risks are you taking? What parts of the journey are you missing out on? Is there something more to life, something included in the trip, that you're not experiencing right now?

One of the first steps you need to take toward discovering personal purpose, and more broadly your lifevision, is to get it on your radar screen. In other words, it's time to start asking the questions, raising your level of awareness about lifevision in general and understanding the relationship between your lifevision and your work. As you gain understanding about your lifevision and its relationship with your work, you'll begin to harness newfound power. You'll appreciate your work in a new way, and experience more satisfaction seven days a week. That is what this book is all about. It is a collection of ideas, stories and tools that will help to guide you in the exploration, discovery and alignment process.

Throughout the book, I'll present a series of diagrams. These illustrations will build upon each other from chapter to chapter, highlighting different aspects of discovery, alignment and renewing of personal lifevision. The first diagram — Your Personal Purpose — illustrates the first component of lifevision.

Lifevision Diagram 1: *Your Personal Purpose*

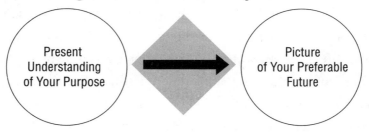

Principle: *Your personal purpose probes the question "Why do I exist?" while at the same time looking to the future and asking, "Where do I want to go?"*

Paradox: *The discovery process can literally take a lifetime; as you advance on the journey, your perspective on purpose changes.*

There are two essential ingredients in personal purpose:
- "Present Understanding of Your Purpose" — this part of the diagram represents your current understanding of your purpose or "why you exist."
- "Picture of Your Preferable Future" — this part of the illustration represents the vision of where you would like to arrive as your future unfolds. It is a specific picture, not a vague notion of what the future might hold.

As you define your life purpose, it will reflect each of these two elements. You will define your present understanding of why you exist. You will also develop a conception of where you would like to go. As you move forward in putting words to your lifevision, it will be important to consider both of these purpose elements.

The paradox of purpose is this: as you advance on the journey, your perspective changes. You are enriched by the experiences of the past and have matured in the process. The events that you encounter become part of your mental and spiritual fabric — part of who you are. As such, your vision of the future will change as life unfolds. The view of your preferable future will evolve to incorporate the new learning you have gained along the way. As Arthur Schopenhauer said, "Our life is like a journey on which, as we advance, the landscape takes on a different view from that which it presented at first, and changes again, as we come nearer."

In this chapter I'll examine why you should take the time to ask the questions about purpose, what personal purpose is all about, and how you can go about discovering your personal purpose.

Why Ask the Questions?

Most of us are wired, in one form or another, with a desire to be significant in some way. We want to make our lives count for something. The famous psychotherapist Maslow told us that significance is one of the basic and universal human needs. Developing a clear sense of purpose is the key to fulfilling your need for significance. While there are certainly other things that contribute to your sense of significance, none is as important as understanding your personal purpose. As you initiate the process of purpose discovery and then dedicate yourself to achieving it, you will begin to experience a measurable significance in your life.

When wrestling with concepts such as purpose, I find a lot of inspiration in the stories of people who have made the world a better place through their work. In reading the personal histories of these people, I am encouraged that it is possible to discover a purpose and make a difference in the lives of people around me. One of history's great examples of a person committed to achieving a purpose through work is Booker T. Washington. In his autobiography *Up From Slavery*, Washington shared his belief that "Providence so often uses men and institutions to accomplish a purpose." It was his steadfast commitment to purpose that gave him the resolve to overcome the numerous obstacles that all African Americans faced in the late 1800's. Fighting the residual effects of his own experiences as a slave, as well as overcoming the incredible prejudice of the time and the scant economic opportunity afforded him, Washington relentlessly pursued his lifevision.

In the midst of his persistence and preparation, the right opportunity was finally afforded him. He recalled, "In May 1881...in a way I dared not expect, the opportunity opened for me to begin my life-work." It was at this time that he was invited to become the head of Tuskegee Institute, a small school for African Americans in Alabama. Henceforth, his life's work — his lifevision — was devoted to "laying of the foundation of the [African American] race through a generous education of the hand, head and heart."

To say the least, his approach to education was novel. He confronted head-on the challenge of providing knowledge to "hundreds of hungry earnest souls" despite the lack of facilities and equipment. He implemented a controversial plan to have the students provide the primary labor in constructing nearly 40 campus buildings. In so doing, Washington's goal was to teach the students "how to lift labour up from mere drudgery and toil, and [that they] would learn to love work for its own sake." Under his leadership, Tuskegee Institute rose from nothing, educating thousands of African-American citizens, imparting hope, and encouraging dreams in the hearts of many.

In recognition of Booker T. Washington's achievements, he was awarded an honorary doctorate by Harvard, the most prestigious university in the country. As he received his degree in June of 1896, Washington shared his understanding of his life experience.

My whole former life — my life as a slave on the plantation, my work in the coal-mine, the times when I was without food and clothing, when I made my bed under a sidewalk, my struggles for an education, the trying days I had at Tuskegee, days when I did not know where to turn for a dollar to continue the work there, the ostracism and sometimes oppression of my race, — all this passed before me and nearly overcame me. I had never sought or cared for what the world calls fame. I have always looked upon fame as something to be used in accomplishing good. I have often said to my friends that if I can use whatever prominence may have come to me as an instrument with which to do good, I am content to have it. I care for it only as a means to be used for doing good.

What a powerful human being. Washington made a commitment — to change the world one person at a time, to overcome adversity in order to fulfill his life-work, and to be an instrument for the common good. In the same way, for you, a lifevision can release newfound power and the resolve to make a difference.

You too can embrace a purpose for your life that will take you to places you never thought possible. In the process, your personal need to be significant, to have made your life count for something, will be fulfilled.

What is Personal Purpose All About?

Wrestling with the meaning of life and the role we play in life's grand scheme is certainly nothing new. People in every age and every culture have searched for an understanding of the big picture and where they fit into that picture. As we collectively reflect on the rebellion of the sixties, the self-centeredness of the seventies, and the conspicuous consumption of the eighties, it becomes evident that even more people in the nineties are seeking something to fill the longing they feel inside.

Increasingly, we are looking for meaning both in our lives and in our work. We're asking the tough questions:

- Why do I exist?
- What is the purpose of my life?
- Is there a master plan of which I am a vital part, or does everything happen by chance?
- Is it possible that I can make the world a better place?
- Do I have a destiny?
- Is it possible to attain fulfillment in my work?
- Are some of the secrets of a meaningful life tied to the discovery of meaning in my work?

In wrestling with these issues, we join billions of others who have searched for an understanding of the meaning of life. When we stand in the shadow of these questions, it's quite normal to experience a real loss for words.

Frankly, it can be a little overwhelming to approach the discovery of personal purpose using only the "big picture" questions like those listed above. Although these questions are important, they are difficult to answer without a more focused starting point. We can begin by looking at four distinct components: (1) your skills, talents and abilities, (2) your personality and temperament, (3) your personal history, and (4) your passions and interests. Together, these four elements make up your personal purpose.

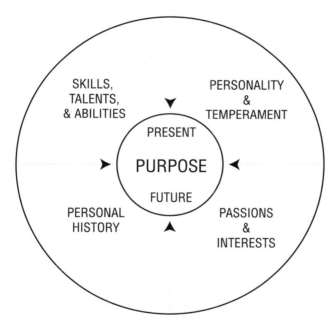

- *Your skills, talents and abilities.*

Carefully taking inventory of your skills, talents and abilities is often the first step in realizing your personal purpose. These are your specific competencies. They include talents like musical ability and the capacity to think logically. They also include the skills that you've acquired through education, training, on-the-job experiences, and so on. Some of your abilities may be more developed than others, and some may even be dormant from years of disuse. It's important to take an accurate inventory of all your competencies, as they will become the nucleus of your personal purpose.

- *Your personality and temperament.*

You are unique, and nowhere is that more apparent than in your personality and temperament. As a teenager, I learned an important lesson from my mother when she told me, "don't deny or try to change your personality." This was a poignant moment for me, full of powerful truth. The way you process life and relate to others is distinctive. You were created with a unique signature, a one-of-a-kind personality and temperament, that can have its fullest expression through your personal purpose.

- *Your personal history.*

Your experiences are incredibly valuable assets, so taking a careful look at past events that have shaped your life makes a lot of sense. Chiseled in stone above the entrance to the National Archives in Washington D.C. is the statement "Past is Prologue." In other words, the past has many lessons for us as we look to our future. Your successes, your failures, and other learning experiences are great tools for helping you determine the focus of your purpose today.

- *Your passions and interests.*

Your personal purpose should include the things that excite, enthuse, and energize you. What do you really want to do? What do you get passionate about? Don't just focus on what others want or expect you to do. Time is too precious to spend all of your working life settling for less, just to have a few years after retirement to finally do what really interests you. Your personal purpose should be integrally linked to your internal desires, interests and passions.

As you evaluate each of these four elements, you should begin to see some emerging themes. These themes are the essence of your personal purpose. The more you reflect on and work through the intentional discovery of personal purpose, the clearer these themes will become. A picture of your personal purpose in the present will begin to emerge. And as your present understanding of purpose becomes clearer, you can begin to envision a picture of your preferable future. You will have a more specific idea of where you would like to go and what it will look like when you get there. As you contemplate what will be necessary to get from where you are now to your vision of the future, you are plotting the course for your success. In fact, the fulfillment of your personal purpose is really synonymous with achieving personal success. Let's take a closer look at what I mean.

Success

Each of us wishes to be successful. I believe it is a genetic trait of the human species to envision our success and to then act upon those visions. But as we accelerate toward making our mark and accomplishing certain goals, have we stopped long enough to catch our breath and ask, "If I achieve what I set out to accomplish, will that qualify as success?" Popular culture offers a lot of examples of what success supposedly is: accumulation of great wealth; achieving stardom in professional athletics; leading an enduring organization; earning $20 million for acting in a motion picture. While each of these may be evidence of success, I don't think any is an adequate definition of success. So what's the right way to think about success?

I don't suppose there's any universally accepted definition of success, but I do believe success is integrally tied to the discovery of personal purpose. In other words, being a success has everything to do with discovering your personal purpose and then living your life with the intention to fulfill that purpose. I've reached this conclusion based on five years of research, extensive contemplation, and protracted discussion with scholars wiser than I am. I'd like to challenge you to think of success this way:

> *Fulfilling your personal purpose,*
> *in relationship with others,*
> *while becoming a person of principle.*

Take a close look at this definition. First, it doesn't require you to achieve some culturally imposed standard for success. Consequently you are free to fulfill your "calling" in a way that is totally unique. How refreshing! Second, the definition reflects the three elements of lifevision — purpose, people and principles. Using the lifevision framework, the standards for measuring your success become (1) whether or not you're actively discovering, aligning, and renewing your purpose — at home, at work, and in the community, (2) whether you're honoring, encouraging, and synergizing with others along the way, and (3) whether or not you're becoming a person of principle and strong character. All along life's journey, then, you can use this three- way test to evaluate your progress towards real success.

This definition of success is simple, straightforward, and it works. Of the many definitions I have seen, it comes closest to an accurate description of what success really is. This definition helps you to focus on your own unique purpose and find fulfillment in a line of work that fits you in particular. You don't have to worry about comparing yourself to Bill Gates, Elizabeth Dole, Michael Jordan, or Mother Teresa. And that is healthy indeed. Others can inspire and encourage us, but we can also get caught up in striving to be someone or something that is not authentically us. The accomplishments of our heroes are uniquely theirs, yet you can be equally successful in the grand scheme of things — by fulfilling your unique purpose and bringing it into alignment with your work. If you can apprehend this truth, it will become one of the most liberating and motivating forces in your life.

My brother Ben awakened me to this way of defining success. Ben is the executive pastor of a thousand-member church in the Midwest. Early in his pastoral career, Ben questioned the personal significance in his role as a full-time pastor. He has many talents, including musical ability, writing and speaking skills, and a special artist's flair. Early on, he wondered if he could make the best use of these talents in the pastorate. He was frustrated from seeing others using their talents, having fun, and earning a much better living.

While wrestling with the decision of whether or not to stay in the pastorate, Ben reflected on the life of Christ. At the end of his life Jesus declared, "I have finished the work I was sent to do." This declaration was in apparent contradiction to the cultural standard of success at the time. Christ didn't accumulate much of anything material, didn't build any kind of organization, was regarded as a rebel and scoundrel by many, and then died a humiliating death. Yet history has proven him to be a great success. His life and teachings have had an impact on billions of people. He was a success because he completed the work he had been sent to do.

During this reflective process, Ben discovered that success was not defined by the accomplishments and experiences of others. Success wasn't measured in comparison to standards of great wealth, outstanding accomplishments, or fame. Rather, he found that success was about fulfilling a unique purpose and having an impact on the lives of others. Ben realized that he was exactly where he was supposed to be — sharing his unique talents and serving others above and beyond selfish motives. Today, Ben brings an unparalleled passion and exuberance to his position as executive pastor. Beloved by people both inside and outside his congregation, he is experiencing the fruits of true alignment with his organization — and, I might add, is a marvelous success.

How Purpose is Discovered

Discovering purpose is one of life's most adventurous undertakings. Once you begin the intentional process of exploring your personal purpose, you'll find yourself on a quest that never really ends.

It's difficult to know where to begin with such a sweeping subject. In my personal coaching efforts, I have found that the following framework is helpful in understanding the main ingredients of the process for discovering purpose.

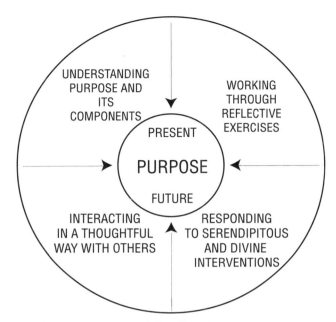

Understanding Purpose and Its Components

The first step in discovering your personal purpose is to gain a general understanding of what purpose is all about. Reading this book is one way to achieve this broad understanding. While this chapter has introduced you to some of the whats and whys of purpose, the other chapters provide much of the context necessary for a more complete picture. Likewise, the Tool Kit exercises at the conclusion of each chapter incorporate several different perspectives on purpose.

As I noted in the Introduction, purpose takes on a much richer meaning when it's considered within the larger framework of lifevision. A common mistake is separation of purpose from the other two critical pieces of the system, people and principles. Physicists have a term for systems such as this — they call them irreducibly complex. What this means is that the system has been reduced to its most basic components and will cease to function if any one of those parts is missing. A common mousetrap, for instance, won't function if any one of its basic parts (the wooden base, the spring, the trip lever, the bait holder) is missing. It is irreducibly complex. Likewise for lifevision, I believe you need all three system components to be fully functional.

Taken as a whole, then, the concepts and practices described in this book will give you the understanding you need to start or continue your journey of discovering personal purpose. As your understanding grows, I'm confident you'll gain even deeper insights about your personal purpose. In turn, these insights will guide you in taking the action necessary to achieve your dreams.

Working Through Reflective Exercises

Just gaining a general understanding about purpose is not enough to make the discovery process work. I encourage you to take the next step by working through the reflective exercises at the end of each chapter. While you might be tempted to skip over the exercises, I would be remiss not to encourage you otherwise. Take the time to reflect and record your answers to these probing questions. To do anything less is sort of like reading the menu, allowing your mouth to water, and then walking out of the restaurant before you've been served the meal. To get the full experience of discovering your lifevision, I encourage you to stick around for the main entrée — do the exercises!

The reflective exercises at the end of this chapter focus on the four distinct elements of purpose: (1) your skills, talents, and abilities, (2) your personality and temperament, (3) your personal history, and (4) your passions and interests. These are really the starting point for the lifevision discovery process. These four exercises are complemented by additional exercises at the end of each chapter which explore many aspects of lifevision and alignment. The more comprehensive and intentional you can be in your discovery process — by working through all of the exercises — the better your sense of purpose will be as a result.

Interacting In A Thoughtful Way With Others

The third component of the purpose discovery process is thoughtful interaction with others. As Chapter 2 will point out, there's something you obtain from interacting with others that you just can't get on your own. In fact, there may be things about yourself that are difficult or impossible for you to see, yet are quite clear to those around you. For instance, a couple of years ago I was unaware how some of my behaviors at work were having an impact on others. While I thought I was coming across as self-confident and assured, I was projecting arrogance and indifference about the opinions of others. It was through the caring reflection of my coworkers that I realized the kind of impression I was really making. For reasons such as this, many organizations have adopted 360-degree feedback programs where the input of subordinates, peers, and superiors is solicited in personnel evaluations. Multiple viewpoints gathered through these types of programs can be especially helpful in improving job performance and in career advancement.

People who you have relationships with — coworkers, family, and friends — bring their own unique perspective to your problems and opportunities. In the discovery of purpose, I find it extremely helpful to involve them at certain key points. These people will have helpful things to say. Not only that, they'll lend you emotional and spiritual support in the process. And that may be even more important!

One way to experience the lifevision discovery process is with a small group of others that you trust. There has been a lot of research about the therapeutic power of small groups — communities, if you will. In this type of setting, you can tap the collective power of many and gain the needed affirmation and strength to explore your personal destiny. I believe in small group communities so strongly that my wife and I have been involved with them for fifteen years now, in one form or another.

The effort of reaching beyond yourself to draw others into the discovery and development of your lifevision is well worth it. I encourage you to give this some serious thought. Are there two or three others that might be able to assist you, even if it's only to answer a few of your questions? Explore your relationships at work and in other arenas. Who might be able to assist you in this process? A respected coworker or personal friend can often provide invaluable advice. I agree that it's more work to do it this way, but you'll be grateful in the end.

Responding to Serendipitous and Divine Interventions

Each of the first three elements of discovering purpose have to do with your proactivity. In other words, you hold the key to making them happen. You need to access the information for understanding what purpose is about, you need to work through the reflective exercises to gain valuable insights, and you need to reach out to your circle of relationships to include them in the discovery process. But this fourth and final step really isn't about you. It's about the serendipitous and divine interventions that grace your life. We all have them — I know because hundreds of you have told me about your experiences.

The intent of this book is not to explore the theological or philosophical basis for the occurrence of divine interventions. I've become sufficiently convinced of their existence by hearing many of your stories and by virtue of my own encounters. Walking away from a crash that involved two vehicles colliding at over 60 miles an hour; my youngest child missed by inches by an oncoming car; receiving an unexpected financial gift from my parents at a most opportune time; getting an inspirational thought one day while I was wandering around Disneyland that ended up saving my company a lot of money — these are just a few of the examples of serendipitous and divine interventions that have come my way.

I'm always on the lookout for these moments. It's not that I'm counting on them to happen, but when they do I want to be able to respond in a positive way. I want to incorporate the occurrence in my understanding of lifevision going forward. I want to learn something and be grateful in the process. And I encourage you to do the same. These special interventions are gifts to you as you discover your personal purpose. How you receive the gifts and react to the circumstances surrounding them may be as important to your personal purpose as all the other things you do in the discovery process.

In review, the four parts of discovering your personal purpose are:

1. Understanding purpose and its components.
2. Working through reflective exercises.
3. Interacting in a thoughtful way with others.
4. Responding serendipitous and divine interventions.

These don't have to happen in sequence. Most likely, it won't happen that way for you, and that's fine. For a compelling discovery process, however, I encourage you to explore each of these avenues.

Personal Purpose: The Destination and The Journey

As you seek to understand your unique purpose and to become successful at fulfilling it, you will encounter the paradox of the destination and the journey. I also like to call this paradox the "dot and the line." To state it in simple terms, the "dot" represents a unique destiny that you have the opportunity to fulfill in your life's journey. A destiny implies a destination — a specific point at which you would like to arrive. It is about focusing on a unique goal and a particular kind of work that will achieve that goal. The "dot," then, is characterized by the elements of specificity, uniqueness, and irreplaceability.

The "line," on the other hand, represents the journey of life and the enjoyment of events along the way. It's about smelling the roses, enjoying the sunset, and admiring the evening chorus of crickets. It's about appreciating the relationships you have and being satisfied with your work, regardless of what type of work it is. The line is more about the enjoyment of the experience rather than the end result. I like to think of the "dot" and "line" as representing two ends of a purpose continuum — with a variety of positions in-between.

The Dot and Line Continuum

The Line — A Journey of Growth

On the right side of the continuum is the line — enjoying the experience of life and sampling the good things that it has to offer along the way. The essence of the line is reflected in this statement by George Bernard Shaw:

> *I rejoice in life for its own sake. Life is no brief candle for me. It's a sort of splendid torch which I've got to hold up for the moment and I want to make it burn as brightly as possible before handing it on to future generations.*

As Shaw points out, the line is about rejoicing in life for its own sake, but it doesn't mean just living for yourself. On the contrary, the line represents a life of personal growth and reaching out to others. It's about finding enjoyment and satisfaction while growing rich in personal character.

In the most complete expression of the line, we could say that the journey *is* the destination. In other words, there is no specific destination per se. There isn't a particular work you need to find nor a special activity to devote yourself to. You can choose to work in any vocation, as each one has its own rewards. You can select any organization to contribute your talents to, as long as you believe in what the organization is doing and you're enjoying yourself in the process.

The Dot — A Destination You're Headed For

On the left side of the continuum is the dot — a specific vision for your life. It is about the fulfillment of something unique and different, most likely through your work. Someone focused on the dot will say, "This is the calling that I have, and I am headed for a specific goal that looks like this..." The person focused on the line says, "I don't sense a particular calling, rather I believe it's more important to enjoy life for its own sake."

One of the best ways to understand the dot is to examine its most radical form of expression. The psychologist Victor Frankl embodied one of the most complete expressions of the dot, as illustrated in the following quotation from his book, *Man's Search for Meaning*:

"Everyone has his own specific vocation or mission in life to carry out a concrete assignment which demands fulfillment. Therein he cannot be replaced, nor can his life be repeated. Thus, everyone's task is as unique as is his specific opportunity to implement it."

Frankl was a prominent psychotherapist practicing in Germany during World War II. With millions of his Jewish comrades, his life was viciously interrupted with a sentence to the

Nazi concentration camps. He was one of the few prisoners allowed to live in exchange for a brutal work detail. While most of the prisoner-workers who had been spared execution were worked to death or took their own lives, a precious few survived. Frankl carefully observed what it was that enabled the small number of prisoners to survive in the midst of the most horrible conditions imaginable. The difference between survival and death, Frankl concluded, was that those who survived had something significant yet to do in their lives — a special purpose that had been yet unfulfilled. It was this compelling personal purpose that gave the survivors the will to live in spite of such wretched circumstances. They knew that the world would be shortchanged if they failed to survive. After the conclusion of the war and his release from Auschwitz, Frankl wrote the book *Man's Search for Meaning*, sharing insights about personal purpose he gained from his experiences in the concentration camp.

In order to really appreciate the radical nature of what Frankl is saying and to understand the "dot" side of the continuum, I think its helpful to take a close look at Frankl's life and the above quote in particular:

- *"Everyone..."*—Frankl explains that each of us, not just a select few, has a calling.

- *"Specific vocation or mission in life to carry out a concrete assignment..."* — Frankl implies that our purpose is more specific than general. He emphasizes the degree of specificity by using the powerful word "concrete." Thus, Frankl tells us that our calling is tangible, solid, and knowable.

- *"Assignment"* — If we have an assignment, it has been given to us by Someone. Frankl implies that a Divine Power has designed a unique calling for us and presented it to us in the form of an assignment.

- *"Therein he cannot be replaced, nor can his life be repeated"* — So as to overstate the point regarding our uniqueness and our special destiny, Frankl says each life is like a fingerprint — it cannot be replicated or replaced.

- *"Thus, everyone's task is as unique as is his specific opportunity to implement it"* — With the final part of the quote, Frankl conveys an important message. Not only is our destiny unique, but the Creator has given us the opportunity to implement it in a totally individual way. We have choices — a whole palette of choices — to express the individuality that is only ours to express.

Can we prove that each life has a dot, a specific destiny? No. However, many of history's greatest achievers were people who had a passion for a very specific purpose. George Washington, Harriet Tubman, Winston Churchill, Marie Curie, Jonathan Edwards, Albert Einstein, Benjamin Franklin, Clara Barton, and Susan B. Anthony were great people devoted to a life of fairly specific purpose.

In examining the lives of these and other great people from history, as well as everyday people we know, we can draw some general conclusions regarding specific purpose. Following are some of the key elements that help explain just what a specific destiny, or a dot, is all about.

- *Fulfilling a specific destiny is the act of living out what you always wanted to do, have felt called to do, or have dreamed about doing.* In reading the biographies of political, business, religious, scientific and scholarly figures, it is apparent that many of these individuals had big dreams about the future. Often, they nurtured these aspirations from a very early age. Winston Churchill, for instance, is known to have exhibited great courage as a teenager because he believed in his future destiny as a great world leader. Oswald Chambers, one of the great theologians of the last two centuries, knew as a youngster that he had a special mission. This phenomenon has many names: a calling, a destiny, a knowing, a big dream, predestination, and so on. This sense of calling or destiny isn't limited to history's great success stories. I've found that it's quite common for everyday people like you and me to experience this same sort of feeling or knowing. While our contributions to humanity may not be as grand as those more famous, we can still make a significant difference in the sphere of relationships around us.

- *As a practical matter, destiny happens at the intersection of opportunity and substantial preparation.* Destiny is not so much about being in the right spot at the right time as it is being persistent and committed. Those with a special sense of purpose have often labored in relative obscurity for years. Only when they are "discovered" does it appear that they were at the right place at the right time. In reality, years of preparation, trial and error, and persistence are behind history's greatest success stories. Thomas Jefferson was fond of saying, "I'm a great believer in luck. And, the harder I work, the more I have of it."

•   *Destiny might be thought of as taking control of life versus life taking control of us.* Instead of reacting to life's events, we actively and optimistically process these events in the frame of our specific purpose. This is the true hallmark of someone with a special sense of destiny. They don't allow the obstacles and challenges of life to push them off course. They turn the tables on circumstances and figure out a way to continue their progress — always in pursuit of a specific vision on the horizon.

•   *Fulfilling destiny requires an exercise of faith as well as taking a certain amount of risk.* There will never be enough evidence in the present to confirm our visions of the future. That means risk will be involved in fulfilling a specific destiny. Many people with such a purpose have "pushed the envelope" of their circumstances to fully apprehend their purpose. They were not content with the status quo. The Wright Brothers worked for years in their pursuit of heavier-than-air flight. There was risk involved in turning their dreams into reality, but they forged ahead anyway, and today we enjoy the fruit of their faith.

The Tension in the Middle of the Paradox

So which is it? Do you have a specific destiny, or is life more of a journey without a specific destination? Certainly, life's seasons reflect both sides of the continuum. But as life ebbs and flows, you will probably be more conscious of the journey than you will a specific destination. That's only natural. It's also possible that you've had an inkling of something more specific, something that was uniquely yours to do. Perhaps you've encountered special touchstones that encouraged you in a profound way to hold onto a dream. If so, you've probably experienced a sort of tension in the middle of the dot and line paradox. Both the dot and the line seem to be valid, and you're not sure which one to hold on to. You want to believe in something unique that you're supposed to do, but you're just as sure that life is to be lived for the experience and not for an end result. That tension is a powerful force that shapes your choices and your view on life.

Maybe you haven't had the slightest inkling of a dot for your life. That's okay. I encourage you to begin pressing toward the dot side of the continuum, at least for a brief period of exploration. You'll find that in pressing toward the dot and daring to ask the questions about a specific purpose for your life, you'll be better off because you did — regardless of the answers you find.

Concluding Thoughts on Purpose

In Robert Falcon Scott's account of his tragic journey to the South Pole in January of 1912, he tells of one occasion when weather conditions were such that a white haze blended with the whiteness of the snow. No horizon was visible. Wherever he looked, it was simply one unbroken whiteness. There was no point in the visible distance upon which they could direct their course as they drove their sledges forward. Before long, they were coming upon their own tracks! Believing they were going forward, they were, in fact, only going around in a great circle. To solve the problem, they began throwing snowballs in the direction of true south so they had something ahead of them on which to fix their eyes.

Few of you will ever lead an expedition to the South Pole, but you really are on a journey. And, like Scott, you need something to fix your eyes on as you move into the future. You want to know that at the end of the journey, your life counted for something — that you didn't just go around in circles. This is what the discovery of your lifevision is all about: digging deep to obtain an understanding of your present and future purpose, reflecting on your relationships and each of the interpersonal roles you play, thinking about your work and how it can be more meaningful. As you undertake the process of asking and answering these questions, your lifevision will begin to take shape. You'll be encouraged and energized about the future. Jesus once said, "Ask and you will receive, seek and you will find, knock and the door will be opened for you." It's time to start asking! Start seeking! Start knocking!

Chapter 1 Tool Kit

Exercise 1-1: Skills, Talents, and Abilities

Your skills, talents, and abilities are integral to your personal purpose. In some areas you may be naturally gifted, while in others you've acquired a particular skill or built upon a core competence. Take the time now to respond to the following questions:

1. What are your natural abilities or talents?

2. What are the specific skills and competencies you have acquired or built upon? List personal disciplines, interpersonal skills, technical competencies, leadership abilities, etc.

3. What other strengths do you have?

4. What qualities do others (especially those closest to you) see in you?

5. What areas have you had the most difficulty with?

6. What have you learned about yourself in the last year? The last five years?

7. In what areas of your life do you feel a sense of destiny?

8. Is there something you used to do quite well, but which you spend little time doing now?

Exercise 1-2: *Personality and Temperament*

Think of your personality and temperament as your internal wiring system. It's the complex array of characteristics, behavior and emotional tendencies, attitudes, traits, and habits that make us who we really are.

1. What parts of your personality do you find positive? Negative?

2. What recharges you?

3. How do you make decisions?

4. If you've taken the Myers-Briggs, DiSC or some other type of personality profile, what did it say about you?

5. How accurate do you think the above profile was in describing the real you?

6. What is significant about how you relate to people?

7. What do others say about your personality?

Exercise 1-3: *Your Personal History*

It's important to look at your personal history as you attempt to understand your personal purpose.

1. Create a personal timeline from date of birth to the present. Indicate on the timeline any significant or memorable events. (See example below.)

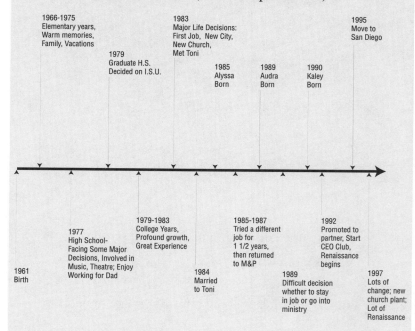

2. As you review your timeline, what significant things stand out? Did you have any periods of major change? What were the key decision moments in your life? Do you see any patterns?

3. Did any events in your childhood significantly impress, change, wound, or inspire you?

4. Where did you receive your early schooling and your early childhood religious training? How did it shape your worldview then and now?

5. Is there anything significant about the life and achievements of your ancestors?

6. Are there any patterns as you examine your bloodline?

7. What are the "power points" in your life? In other words, what major decision points or events have had a significant impact on you?

8. Were you particularly good at something as a youngster?

9. In what period of your life have you experienced the most change?

10. Has the geographic area of your upbringing (i.e. the deep south, the northwest, etc.) affected your worldview and beliefs about life and your future?

11. As a youngster, you always dreamed about being...

Exercise 1-4: Your Passions and Interests

These are the things that excite, enthuse and energize you. What do you really want to do? Your personal purpose should be integrally linked to your internal desires and interests.

1. What lights you up?

2. In what area of your life do you have the most energy? What gives you the most pleasure?

3. If you knew you couldn't fail, what one thing would you do?

4. In 5 or 10 years, what do you want to be doing with your life?

5. When you look at your life, what activities are of the greatest worth?

6. What are the interests or activities that you really enjoy doing or that excite you the most?

7. When do you feel most full of joy?

Chapter 2

Life is Not a Solo Flight

"In a difficult and fractured and complex world, in problems of failure and of success, but especially in the joys and tragedies of our personal lives, we touch each other. This 'touching' is at the heart of who we are."

—Max DePree, *Leadership is an Art*

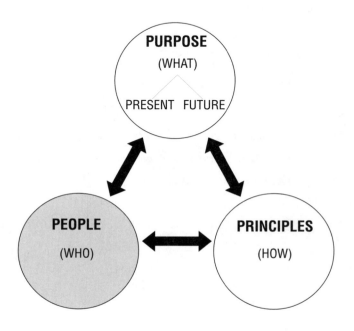

I love rags-to-riches stories, or any story of someone who has achieved success through hard work and ingenuity. One thing bothers me, however. How many times have we been told how these people are a shining example of the "self-made" man or woman? Probably more often than I can recount.

But is there really such a thing as the self-made man or woman? I don't think so. In reality, all of us are a product of parental influence, family systems, educational systems, the media, and organized religion, to name a few. To put it another way, our talents and gifts, our system of thought and our capacity to serve, have all been shaped by others. We've been influenced and affected by the individuals who took the time to care for, teach, and love us.

Consider this story about Sandra Day O'Connor as told in *Bringing Out the Best In People*:

The Lazy B Ranch is comprised of 260 square miles of scrub brush on the New Mexico and Arizona border and has been in the Day family since 1881. When Harry and Ada Mae Day were ready to have their first child, they traveled 200 miles to El Paso for the delivery, and Ada Mae brought her baby, Sandra, home to a difficult life. The four-room adobe house had no running water and no electricity. One would have thought that with such limited resources, Sandra's intellectual future was slim.

But Harry and Ada Mae were dreamers who did not allow themselves to be limited by their surroundings. Harry had been forced by his father's death to take over the ranch rather than enter Stanford University, but he never gave up hope that his daughter would someday study there. And Ada Mae continued to subscribe to metropolitan newspapers and to magazines such as Vogue *and* The New Yorker. *When Sandra was four, her mother started her on the Calvert method of home instruction and later saw that she went to the best boarding schools possible. Sandra's brother Alan said that one summer their parents packed them in the car and they drove to all the state capitals west of the Mississippi. "We climbed to the dome of every building until finally we had to come home," he said.*

Sandra did go to Stanford, then on to law school, and eventually on to become the first woman Supreme Court justice in the United States. On the day of her swearing in, the Day family was there, of course. During the ceremony Alan watched her closely as she put on her robe, then walked to her seat among the justices. "She looked around, saw the family and locked her eyes right into ours," said Alan. "That's when the tears started falling."

What causes a woman like Sandra Day O'Connor to go so far? Intelligence, of course. And lots of inner drive. But much of the credit goes to a determined little ranch woman sitting in her adobe house at night, reading to her children hour after hour, and to parents scampering up the stairways of capitol domes, their children in tow.

(Reprinted from *Bringing Out The Best In People*,
by Alan Loy McGinnis, copyright © 1985
Augsburg Publishing House. Used by permission of Augsburg Fortress.)

Our personal purpose is always enriched and influenced by others. Life is not a solo flight. We're on the planet to interact with others in meaningful relationships, with the intent to accomplish something and to make the world a better place.

Yet something inside us may chafe at the thought that our personal purpose is fulfilled in relationship with, in connection to, and by joint efforts with others. We may prefer to think of ourselves as successful individuals in our own right, self-made men and women. But this is shallow thinking. In reality, it is our efforts with, through, and for others that help us to experience true success.

Lifevision Diagram 2: *Lifevision Communities*

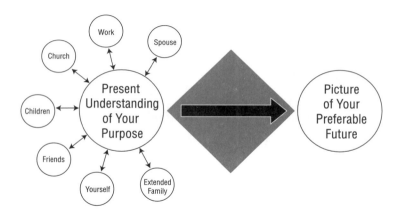

Principle: *Lifevision is fulfilled with and through other people.*
Paradox: *You are the one that must make the choices that determine your destiny.*

This illustration builds on the basic diagram in Chapter 1. I've added the element of "lifevision communities" surrounding your present understanding of personal purpose. This chapter will explore the interrelationship of our purpose with others. An accurate understanding of each of your lifevision communities is essential to understanding your personal purpose.

In fact, you cannot separate an understanding of personal purpose from an understanding of your lifevision communities. All of life is experienced with and through our relationships with others. As such, our personal purpose is not something apart from our present key relationships. Rather, it is closely tied to those relationships. Said another way, each of our our lifevision communities has an impact on our personal purpose in a unique way. Likewise, we have an impact on the people in our lifevision communities. It's this two-way, dynamic interaction that can make the experience of personal purpose so rich.

Our purpose is certainly found in the context of our relationships. However, the ultimate responsibility for achieving your life purpose rests with you. You are the one who must confront the tough choices that will have an impact on your future. To delegate your decisions or to permit others to make choices for you is to forfeit your privilege and your responsibility to shape your own future.

So, when do you act individually and when do you reach out to others? That is the paradox. On the extreme ends of the continuum, there is trouble lurking: we can become self-absorbed and egotistical, or we can become overly reliant on others. Neither of these is healthy, so we need to find a sweet spot in the middle.

Tony and Cindy's Story

While writing this book, I witnessed the phenomenon of life-vision communities affecting purpose. Tony and Cindy's story illustrates the meaningful interaction that lifevision communities have on our personal purpose, and how the conflict between these elements can produce a healthy tension.

Tony is a key person on the consulting team that I lead in San Diego. He and his wife relocated here from the Midwest about one-and-a-half years ago. Things had been progressing fairly well when the arrival of their first baby presented a new set of challenges. In particular, Tony and Cindy began to wonder about moving back home.

The normal methodology for working through a decision of this nature is to list the pros and the cons of making the move back to the Midwest. Once you have all the things listed, you see which side of the paper has the longer list. I have seen countless people process their decisions precisely this way — weighing the pluses and minuses of things such as monetary concerns, career advancement opportunities, climate and recreational amenities, the presence of family, etc.

I suggested that Tony consider a slightly different perspective in making a decision. I challenged him to consider the specific purpose for his life and the lifevision communities surrounding that purpose. I challenged both Tony and Cindy to consider which lifevision communities (relationships) — those in San Diego or those back in the Midwest — would best facilitate the accomplishment of his personal purpose. In other words, I was asking

Tony to put his personal purpose and his lifevision communities at the center of his decision.

It was a tough decision. On one hand, there was a loving family and a lot of supportive friends for them back in the Midwest. This was no small factor. Many of us can relate to the warmth and pleasure of being surrounded by loving family members. This seems particularly heightened when a new baby is factored into the equation. On the other hand, there was the prospect of serious professional and personal opportunities on the West Coast. Although some of Tony and Cindy's lifevision communities in San Diego were not nearly as well developed as their extended family community in the Midwest, there were considerable benefits to remaining in San Diego. Which to choose?

Each of Tony and Cindy's lifevision communities influenced their decision, yet they ultimately had to make the choice themselves. They were the ones who would live with the consequences — both positive and negative — of their decision. It was a fascinating process to watch. The principle of lifevision communities and the paradox of making the final choice was happening right in front of me! In the end, they made the joint decision to commit to the West Coast for a period of years and to reevaluate at some point down the road.

Tony and Cindy were able to focus on their decision by exploring two key questions:

- "What is my personal purpose?"
- "In the overall scheme of things, which relationships are the key to facilitating the advancement of my personal purpose?"

These are the questions we each need to ask ourselves. Let's explore how to go about it.

Your Lifevision Communities and Your Purpose

Understanding how lifevision communities are part of your purpose starts with taking a close look at each of them. Your lifevision communities are sets of specific interpersonal relationships you are presently involved in. Most of you have a lifevision community list that looks something like this:

- You and Yourself
- You and Your Work
- You and Your Spouse
- You and Your Children
- You and Your Extended Family
- You and Your Spiritual or Social Organization
- You and Your Close Friends

Each of these lifevision communities plays an important role. Few of us take the time, however, to ask, "What communities am I a part of?" and "What role does each community play in fulfilling my purpose?" They are very deliberate questions, and though we may not be comfortable in asking them, that is precisely what we need to do.

You and Yourself

The first lifevision community is a subtle one, and is often overlooked: the community of You and Yourself. That is, each of us has a relationship with ourselves first. We must know ourselves — our strengths and weaknesses, our likes and dislikes. It is important to evaluate the health of our relationship with ourselves. Do we know ourselves that well? What do others say about us? Do we agree? Is there a measure of health and stability inside us, or do we feel insecure and troubled? If you feel or see a number of trouble spots in this lifevision community, then a fair amount of work needs to be done before moving much further. A strong foundation of self-awareness, self-esteem and self-love will give you the capacity to build healthy relationships with your other lifevision communities.

In getting to the root of your relationship with yourself, it might be helpful to consider your different personal dimensions: mind, emotions, body, and spirit. Each of these elements reveals different aspects about you. Together, they comprise the authentic you. To look at only one or two dimensions won't give you the complete picture. Many people aren't comfortable probing some areas of the mind, emotion, and the spirit; yet these are precisely the dimensions that need examining! When you begin to gain a deeper understanding of who you are, you experience life in a much richer fashion.

Time spent in developing each of our personal dimensions will pay off handsomely in our other lifevision communities. To the degree that we're personally healthy, we'll bring life and vitality to our other roles. This is one of the real delights of tending to my own personal dimensions. Each week, I focus on strengthening each of my personal arenas. Whether it's physical exercise, reflective quiet time, or reading an intriguing book, I'm always looking to expand the boundaries of each personal dimension. As a result, I find I'm able to have something to give to others, whether it be an attentive attitude toward a coworker's problem, a depth of conversation with my spouse, or a spiritual challenge for a church group. I can bring these gifts to my relationships because I've made the effort to be healthy in my relationship with myself.

I hope you don't get the impression that everything flows smoothly for me in my relationship with myself. Although I've experienced some personal victories, this is the lifevision community where my most intense struggle takes place. For instance, I have real difficulty keeping my emotions on an even keel. I get angry and impatient easily, and those closest to me suffer the consequences. At work, I'm never satisfied until whatever I'm working on is perfect. I'm probably harder on myself than I am on any of my coworkers. This perfectionist flaw has cost me a lot of time and energy, and it's something I'm always working on. There are a lot of other examples of the challenges I'm dealing with on a personal level, just like you. I'll explore these challenges in greater detail in Chapters 7 and 8.

You and Your Work

One of the most important lifevision communities is the relationship between you and your work. Some experts estimate that we spend approximately sixty percent of our time at work or getting ready for it. Because of this fact, the lifevision community of You and Your Work is usually the most integrally linked to your life purpose. You shouldn't compromise in this important arena of your life. Unfortunately, that's what many of us end up doing.

There are any number of ways to view work: as a way to pay the bills, as a stepping stone to something else, as the thing that happens in between weekends, and so on. The more narrow views of work are part of the "Thank God It's Friday" phenomenon so prevalent today. In short, work is rarely the fulfilling experience it should be. It's just a job. We look to the weekends for relief from the drudgery. But the TGIF approach shortchanges the rewarding experience that work can be — if it is aligned with your life purpose and if you are aligned with your organization. That is the reason you picked up this book — to explore how this is done.

It might be helpful for you to look at work from four different perspectives held by different members of the workforce:

- *Work as a Job* — This may be the most common view of work. Unfortunately, it is the most narrow and unfulfilling of the four. At this level, work is something you do because you have to. You do it to pay bills and to provide for your family.

- *Work as an Occupation* — At this level, work is seen as something more than just a job. It is an important part of life, but not necessarily one in which you grow and develop. Work as an occupation involves some sense of fulfillment and accomplishment, but stops short of what it could be.

- *Work as a Career* — This perspective views work as something more meaningful and significant than either of the first two. Another name for "work as a career" is profession. Here, work is important to you. You diligently seek to grow and to improve your skills and abilities. Work provides an appreciable psychic and emotional, as well as economic, income.

- *Work as a Vocation* — At this level, work is the fulfillment of your calling, your unique destiny. Vocation is derived from the Latin word *vocare* meaning *to call*. Viewing work through the lens of vocation means you are looking to "self-actualize" at the most meaningful level.

The above perspectives are all valid views of work. In some respects, you can experience alignment of your personal purpose and your work at any level. You can also experience alignment of yourself with your company at any of the four levels. However, as you probably surmised, the likelihood of alignment (both between your purpose and your work, and you and your company) increases with each successive level. That is because the lifevision community of You and Your Work elevates in meaning and significance as you progress through the perspectives.

I've always had an intuitive sense of aligning my life purpose with my work, and myself with my employer. I've never wanted to waste time just "earning a living" while I could be "making a life." I haven't always seen my work as my vocation, however. Earlier in my professional life, I would characterize my viewpoint as somewhere between occupation and career. Over time, my view has matured and changed. In the last five years, I have had much more of a sense of vocation. Hence, I have become very focused on the discovery of my specific purpose and the alignment of that purpose with both my work and the organization I work for.

Throughout this five-year journey I have spent countless hours studying the topic, interviewing others, observing the behaviors of my clients and associates, and pushing the boundaries of my own experience. As I have actively sought to discover my life purpose and align it with my work, I have faced many challenges and met with much frustration. Part of the difficulty I've encountered is that alignment is a fairly new concept in the business world. Many organizations are just now beginning to understand the importance of alignment and what it means to their future.

Does everyone need to see their work as a career or vocation? No. Does everyone need to be heading in that direction? No. As I said, you can experience the alignment of yourself with your work and alignment with your employer at any level. However, it may be more difficult for you to reach alignment if you view work as a job or occupation. The choice is up to you. You have to decide the most meaningful relationship between your personal purpose and your work.

You and Your Spouse

For those of you who are married or involved in a serious relationship, this is the most natural lifevision community to look at next. How would you evaluate the health of your most intimate relationship? Are the communication lines open and honest? Is there a vitality to the relationship? Is passion evident? Is there a commitment to the long term? To what extent does this relationship help you to nurture and to grow in your life purpose?

Many people experience problems with this lifevision community. Men in particular tend to isolate their spouses from their work and hence their life purpose. This can be a major mistake. I've found that I need to be more deliberate about sharing my work with my wife, Toni. Likewise, I want to be drawn into her world.

It can be very rewarding to involve the person with whom you are most intimate in the development of your life purpose. Who better to share our hopes and dreams? Who better to help us see who we really are? These are the people who encourage us to "go for it" when the times get tough. They assuage our bruised egos in moments of defeat and share the triumph of our accomplishments.

Indeed, sharing my journey — my purpose — with a soul-mate has been one of the profound joys of my life. In the context of a lifelong relationship with Toni, I have been challenged, excited, encouraged, and, most of all, loved. There is a richness beyond words to a relationship like this. It is a blending of two spirits, unified in a life purpose.

You and Your Children

Children can be both a challenging and a rewarding lifevision community. Our children are in many ways our most tangible legacy. They represent an embodiment of ourselves, yet are completely individual. We want to hold on to them for as long as we can, yet we are anxious to see them become independent and successful.

Children can be integral to the fulfillment of your life purpose. A strong commitment to raising your children with love and care can positively affect your other lifevision communities as well. During the eighteen or so years that they spend with us, our children have a tendency to challenge us with every conceivable problem. It is in working through these challenges that we learn invaluable lessons for fulfilling our life purpose.

In particular, effectiveness at work can be enhanced by the trials of parenting. Children teach you to be a better communicator, to practice what you preach, to be fair to others, and so on. All of these parenting lessons carry over into our relationships with coworkers and team members in the work environment. For example, one of the key mistakes I make at work is explaining things with insufficient detail. I make the assumption that the person I'm talking to understands what I really want. My daughters Alyssa, Audra, and Kaley have taught me that I need to be more explicit when I'm communicating. I have learned to slow down, to be completely clear about my expectations, and to make fewer assumptions, both at home and at work.

My relationship with my daughters has also added a deep sense of joy to my life purpose. It is one of the truly rewarding elements of life's journey to interact with my children. They have taught me to appreciate the journey a little more and to see the simplicity in things. They remind me that there's always a tomorrow to correct a mistake I made today, and that I should never take myself too seriously.

As my wife and I invest time with each of our children, the payback in emotional satisfaction is great. Yes, there is a lot of effort and frustration inherent in raising children. But the opportunity to instill in them a sense of purpose, a commitment to core values, and a loving attitude toward others is a rewarding and satisfying experience.

A note of caution is appropriate here. We sometimes make decisions that run counter to the long-term well being of our children. A decision to divorce, to relocate, to overcommit to work, to travel extensively, or to go overboard on our personal recreation — each of these can have substantive adverse effects on our children. It's important, in this lifevision community as well the others, to be aware of the full impact of the decisions we're making.

You and Your Extended Family

The mobility of our population over the last three decades has produced profound changes in our interactions with extended families. In less mobile eras, extended families often helped to raise children, worked together in the family business, celebrated holidays and birthdays, and attended the same church. Today there is often a number of physical miles between parents, grandparents, siblings, and other relatives that prevent us from enjoying these sorts of things.

Although mobility, divorce, and remarriage have changed the way we relate to our extended families, they still play important roles in our life purpose. It may be more difficult to maintain that same degree of closeness today, yet it is no less important than in past times.

I highly value my relationships with my extended family members, most of whom live in the Midwest. My wife and I make special efforts to bridge the gap of miles between us and to keep our families close despite the distance. These efforts are rooted in a deep sense of love for our families, but also in the belief that these relationships are important in accomplishing our life purpose. For example, in considering the move that we made to San Diego a couple of years ago, some of the best counsel came from our family. Though they didn't want to see us go, they encouraged us to do what would be most beneficial in fulfilling our purpose.

We have worked hard at maintaining these important relationships. It's obvious that the connection our daughters feel with their grandparents, uncles, aunts, and cousins is a very meaning-ful part of their lives. It's fun to watch the anticipation and excite-ment build in the weeks before going home for Christmas or summer vacation. Just recently, I spied over Alyssa's shoulder as she jotted down some personal thoughts on "why Christmas is an exciting time." Her list included "presents, family celebration, going to Illinois, cousins, good food, staying at Grandma's..." Yes, our lifevision community of extended family is vital to our lives, even if that family is two thousand miles away.

Not everyone, of course, has the same degree of appreciation for their extended family. If you find yourself wanting to create a little distance from family, you're certainly not alone. Although it isn't necessary for everyone to maintain a vital link to their blood relatives, perhaps it's time to mend a broken relationship or to extend forgiveness for a wrong that's been done. You never know what's on the other side of a restored relationship!

How important is your extended family to you? How impor-tant are these relationships to helping you achieve your goals? Do you need to be in close geographic proximity to them, or is it more important for you to be where you are? Regardless of how you feel about family, it's critical to ask these questions. If you're like me, you'll need to determine what it will take to nurture com-munication in spite of the miles of physical separation.

You and Your Spiritual or Social Organization

Precisely because of the geographic distance between us and our extended family members, many of us have sought out and found new "families" where we live. These families often come in the form of a church, temple, or some type of social or service organization. Involvement in these kinds of groups can be a refreshing and healthy part of your life.

Spiritual and social organizations provide us with a sense of belonging, as well as a place to exercise talents that we can't express through our other lifevision communities. They help us to grow and develop spiritually as well as emotionally and mentally. The balance provided by churches, charitable institutions, and social networks is invaluable, allowing us to become involved with something bigger than ourselves. The lessons we learn can be critical to the enrichment of our life purpose.

In 1997, our family had the once-in-a-lifetime opportunity to be part of a brand new "church plant." We helped to start a church in an area of San Diego with a very low ratio of churches to the surrounding population. This experience was filled with many challenges, especially for our children. As we devoted a fair amount of energy and resources to making the church plant successful, each member of our family discovered something new about themselves. We were all stretched and challenged in a positive way. By investing in the community and people around us, we've received a meaningful gift of personal growth and development in return.

You and Your Close Friends

It's always important to leave time in our busy schedules for just being with friends and neighbors, the relationships that don't necessarily have any type of task element attached. How important are these social relationships to you?

Although we seem to have our hands full with the other lifevision communities, my wife and I try to set aside some time to spend with friends and neighbors. Sometimes it seems that we're too busy to take the time to socialize, and that can be a mistake!

Our move to San Diego gave us a unique opportunity to interact with a group of new neighbors, coworkers, and fellow church members. While enjoying the richness of building new relationships, we've also tried hard to maintain the friendships we left behind in the Midwest. As the kids' song goes, "Make new friends but keep the old, one is silver and the other gold."

The Role of Others in Increasing Our Self-Awareness

In a comprehensive study involving thousands of people over several years, the Center for Creative Leadership compiled information about the characteristics of effective leaders. The study concluded that one of the key attributes of being an effective leader is being self-aware. An individual who clearly understands his or her strengths, weaknesses, opportunities, and limitations is in a powerful position. A strong foundation of self-awareness allows you to capitalize on your strengths, compensate for your weaknesses, and leverage your best opportunities into reality. On the other hand, lacking self-awareness can result in serious trouble.

I'm sure you know someone who is not self-aware, or at least not as aware as they could be. These people seem to have a higher opinion of themselves than others do. They frequently make remarks that cause us to say "who do they think they're kidding?" They also tend to leave behind a trail of failure and hurt. Until someone is bold enough to speak the truth, they usually continue this pattern of dysfunctional behavior.

The truth is that we all have blind spots. It's easy to deceive ourselves by saying, "I'm okay." But that type of thinking is a subtle trap, one that ultimately leads to stagnation and dysfunction. We need to open up, to allow the flashlight of truth to shine on and expose these blind spots within us. Personal growth always starts with increasing our self-awareness.

How does this happen? How do we get the flashlight of truth to do its work? By seeking out the input and assistance of others. Those we respect and care about help us to focus on the things that need changing as well as those strengths upon which we should build. The healthiest people I know are involved in open, accountable relationships where there is a free and caring exchange of truth. For instance, your boss or supervisor can offer insight into behaviors you need to change in order to better your performance. Likewise, work peers can provide constructive criticism. It is in the context of open relationships like these that discrepancies between our walk and our talk can be brought to light.

Being a part of accountable relationships has been a key part of my life in the last decade. The examples of how others have held the mirror of self-awareness up to me are endless. For example, my wife and I are committed to an open, honest dialogue. I must confess that she is better at this kind of communication than I am. It is through her loving honesty that I have confronted some of my worst demons. It has made our fifteen year relationship rich and full. My brother Ben has also been a powerful force in my life, challenging and encouraging me. My work colleagues, John, Bob, and Tony, are always motivating me to make the best use of my time and talents. Each of these open relationships has shaped and had an impact on the person I am today.

Perhaps the most powerful form of self-awareness comes through our relationship with God. This can be an incredibly challenging and meaningful relationship. Indeed, the flashlight that the Creator uses can reveal the most painful truth, but here we also receive encouragement in our quest for growth and the hope for a brighter and better future.

Concluding Thoughts on Lifevision Communities

Your life is a mosaic of relationships, each adding new textures and diversity to your lifevision. As I conclude this chapter, I want to challenge you with a final thought. What is the motive at the heart of your lifevision communities — in relating to, working with, and experiencing life with others? Is your motive one of service and love, or are you more interested in preserving your own self-interest?

There's a proverb that goes something like this: "As you lose your life for others, you end up saving it in the process." Many philosophers and authors have explored this puzzling paradox. In the last ten years or so, I've noticed a resurgence of interest in this truth, particularly in business circles. Much of this philosophy is embodied in the modern "servant leader" movement. Valuable contributions to the exploration of this "lost life" principle have been made by Peter Block in *Stewardship*, Stephen Covey in *Principled Centered Leadership*, Robert Greenleaf in *The Servant Leader*, Laurie Beth Jones in *Jesus, CEO*, James Autry in *Love and Profit*, Max DePree in *Leadership is an Art*, and Rushworth Kidder in *Shared Values for a Troubled World*.

What these scholars, as well as many of history's great thinkers, have told us is this:

It is in serving others — giving away, or losing, our life—
with the motive of increasing others' well being,
that we will find true fulfillment and satisfaction,
and hence, find our life.

If, on the other hand, we pursue self-interest as our primary motive, we can be assured that fulfillment and satisfaction will remain elusive goals. As you press on with the lifevision discovery process, I encourage you to consider these profound truths.

Chapter 2 Tool Kit

Exercise 2-1: *Lifevision Communities, Definition and Examination*

Use the following table to define each of your present life-vision communities and what they mean to you.

Lifevision Community	How important is this lifevision community to me? How can this community help me achieve my purpose?	How much energy and attention am I giving to this lifevision community? Is it the right amount?	How can I personally improve this lifevision community? Do I need to do something differently?
You and yourself			
You and work			
You and spouse			
You and children			
You and extended family			
You and church, temple, social or community organization			
You and your close friends			
You and...			

Exercise 2-2: *Increasing Your Self-Awareness*

Complete the following questions, each of which is designed to help you examine your strengths and weaknesses.

1. Reflect on one of your past successes. Describe the events that led to the success. What does this success tell you about yourself? What lesson for the future can you learn from this?

2. Reflect on one of your past failures. Describe the events that surrounded the failure. How did it happen? What does this failure tell you about yourself? What lesson for the future can you learn from this?

3. How would others describe your key strengths?

4. What is it about your strengths that tends to get you in trouble? What lesson can you learn from this?

5. What have you done in the past to develop and capitalize on your strengths?

6. How would others describe your weaknesses?

7. What have you done in the past to overcome areas of weakness?

Chapter 3

hat's Your Worldview?

(And Why Does it Matter?)

Truth Never Dies

Truth never dies. The ages come and go.
The mountains wear away, the stars retire.
Destruction lays earth's mighty cities low;
And empires, states and dynasties expire;
But caught and handed onward by the wise,
Truth never dies.

Though unreceived and scoffed at through the years;
Though made the butt of ridicule and jest;
Though held aloft for mockery and jeers,
Denied by those of transient power possessed,
Insulted by the insolence of lies,
Truth never dies.

It answers not. It does not take offense.
But with a mighty silence bides its time;
As some great cliff that braves the elements
And lifts through all the storms its head sublime,
It ever stands, uplifted by the wise,
And never dies.

As rests the Sphinx amid Egyptian sands;
As looms on high the snowy peak and crest;
As firm and patient as Gibraltar stands,
So truth, unwearied, waits the era blessed
When men shall turn to it with great surprise.
Truth never dies.

—Author Unknown

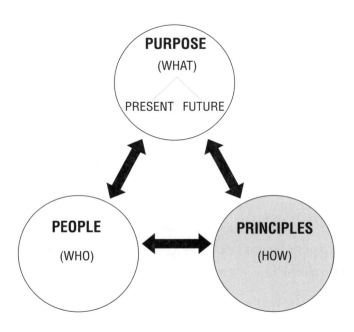

What is your worldview, and why is it important in the discovery of your lifevision? Your worldview is a collection of core beliefs about how the world works and, specifically, how you make sense of all that happens around you. You may not spend a lot of time thinking about your worldview. You may even think you don't have one. But everyone does, regardless of whether or not it has been articulated. Assessing your worldview is one of the key steps in the discovery of your lifevision. A clear sense of what you're about and where you're headed is integrally linked to your worldview.

Why is something that you probably don't give much conscious thought to so important in the discovery and definition of your life purpose? It has to do with roots. Remember Alex Haley's *Roots*, the best-selling book and popular television miniseries of the 1970's? In order to understand his present and future circumstances, the author traced his ancestral beginnings. His intense examination of where he had come from lead to an understanding of who he was and where he was going. Likewise for you, it is important to examine your basic underlying framework — your worldview, the roots behind why you believe and act as you do.

Lifevision Diagram 3: *Core Principles and Your Worldview*

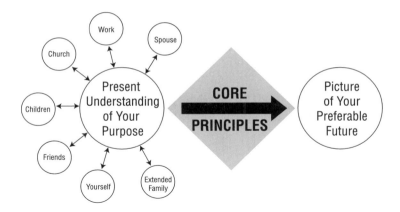

Principle: *There are a set of core principles, proven true over time, which are the baseline for a successful life.*

Paradox: *Your worldview may or may not align with core principles, and may even obscure your understanding of them.*

This illustration adds two new elements to the diagram from Chapter 2. One is the addition of Core Principles in the background. Core principles, according to best-selling author Stephen Covey, are the fundamental laws of human relationships. They are sort of like the air we breathe — ever-present and necessary to sustain life, yet hardly noticed, talked about, or consciously considered. Core principles are just as real as the physical and chemical laws which govern the universe. In essence, they define the atmosphere in which we execute purpose and live out our relationships. If we can discover and apply them, we should be able to build a successful life.

The other addition to the diagram is your worldview, which is at the center of how you think and perceive yourself. This includes your conception of personal purpose. Your worldview is a collection of beliefs that influences how you view life. It affects every decision you make and every behavior you engage in.

It is in the relationship between worldview and core principals that an interesting paradox enters the picture. Your worldview may or may not align with core principles, and may even obscure your understanding of them. It's this paradox that is at the heart of one of life's major challenges: how can you change your worldview, and your behavior, to bring it into alignment with core principles? In other words, how do you become an authentic person of principle? The answers to this question can have a significant influence on your lifevision.

In probing this interesting arena, I've broken this chapter into the following key sections:
- *What are core principles?*
- *What is your worldview?*
- *Is there a gap between core principles and your worldview?*
- *What can you do to close the gap?*

What are core principles?

In the postmodern era, to suggest that there is such a thing as core principles — universal and timeless truths — is a fairly outrageous notion to many. Our pluralistic culture has called into question the existence of objective principles or absolute truths. Society says that there is no officially approved pattern of belief or conduct. All ideas and conventions are to be equally tolerated because they are all equally valid and true. Pluralism emphasizes that life is much like climbing a mountain; there are many roads to the top and the means by which we traverse those roads are all equally valid. There are no axioms of human relationships. But is truth a matter of personal preference? Is everything relative?

Although many modern thinkers have dispensed with the notion of universal truths, history is full of thousands who have thought otherwise. The founders of the United States of America declared, "We hold these truths to be self evident..." In fact, they constructed an entire Constitution of law based on certain underlying truths — laws of human relationships — which they believed transcended the time and culture in which they lived. Indeed, over two hundred years later, those same truths are the basis for our country's moral and legal code.

Take a closer look at some of history's major figures. Martin Luther King, Jr., for instance, devoted himself to the singular cause of justice and equality for African-American citizens. He believed that this cause, his life purpose, was in direct alignment with the principles that govern all human relationships. Abraham Lincoln also pursued his destiny within the framework of a higher calling and in cooperation with a deeply held set of principles. Mother Teresa spent her life caring for thousands of needy people because of an intense belief in an operative set of higher principles. In fact, most people whom we consider successful were committed to an enduring set of principles within which their life purpose was fulfilled.

What about an example from the business arena? I particularly like the story of J.C. Penney, founder of the retail chain that bears his name. Mr. Penney was committed to a set of core truths that he believed governed all human interactions. He named his first store "The Golden Rule Store" because of what he believed to be the most important rule for success in business: "Treat others with the same respect that you want to be treated." The credo of Penney's retail operation was "a fair remuneration and not all the profit the traffic will bear." He established systems within the company to ensure that its associates engaged in principle-centered business practices, honoring employees and customers alike. Though he faced incredibly hard times — he lost his entire $40 million fortune in the Depression — he was committed to a life of principle.

The list of leaders who practiced and taught behaviors based on core truths goes on. Moses, Gandhi, Aristotle and Jesus Christ all shared one thing in common: a belief in the existence of certain core truths which transcended culture, ethnic origin, religion, and every other human differentiator.

I strongly believe that there are indeed core principles that are not dependent on our experience or relative to the times or circumstances we're facing. Core principles haven't changed from one season or century to the next. They are timeless and unchanging. The fact that principles are objective makes their discovery and application no less of an adventure. In fact, it's downright difficult. We aren't going to crack the secrets of the meaning of life in a moment's time and then quickly pass on to more enjoyable tasks. This journey is a lifelong endeavor.

In my attempt to define some core principles, I've come up with the following list:

- **Respect yourself and others.** All people are valuable and deserve to be treated with respect, dignity, and fairness. Success is built upon treating others as you want to be treated. Live "The Golden Rule."

- **Build trust through win-win solutions.** Seeking a mutually beneficial outcome for all interpersonal relationships is the cornerstone of trust.
- **Integrate and balance your life.** You will excel when you are balanced and seek success in all areas of your lives. Achievement in one area cannot compensate for failure or neglect in other areas.
- **Let your walk match your talk.** Honesty, sincerity, and integrity provide the foundation for leadership, cooperation, and success.
- **Accept personal responsibility for change.** Change happens from the inside out. Choose to take responsibility for your own attitude and actions.
- **Work together.** We can achieve far more working together than we can individually. Full effectiveness requires a free exchange of ideas. Strategy and problem solving works best when we tap into the genius and insights of all.
- **Advance with a lifevision.** Personal fulfillment comes when you discover your unique purpose and devote yourself to fulfilling it in association with others.
- **Never stop learning.** Growth comes from learning as you risk, fail, and succeed.
- **See challenges as opportunities.** Change, disruption, and challenges in your environment provide new opportunities for growth and success.
- **Persist and it will pay off.** You will eventually reap what you sow. Ultimate success requires persistent integrity, hard work, learning, and change.

Although the above list is far from complete and is probably not the purest expression of each core principle, I've found these examples to be very useful. These truths have stood the tests of time and experience, across all cultures, religions, and schools of thought. The next step is to examine your own worldview to see how it compares.

What is your worldview?

Every kind of systemic thought — whether it's chemistry, sociology, physics, mathematics, architecture, or religion — begins with a framework. These disciplines all begin by taking something for granted. In other words, there are certain truths upon which the remaining premises are built. For instance, the development of science as we know it would have been impossible without the belief that the universe is rational, even though this cannot be factually proven. Each field of science takes certain presupposed "givens" and builds upon them. Just like the science of physics, your parenting style, your work habits, your religious behavior, and your approach toward relationships are all rooted in a collection of presupposed beliefs known as your worldview. Your core beliefs represent what you accept as "true" as you relate to the outside world. Not all of the ideas and beliefs in your worldview are necessarily provable or factual. They are the things you accept as true about life, based on your diverse experiences.

As you experience life, you add to and subtract from your worldview. Your parents shaped and formed your first version of a worldview. As you became more aware of the world, certain key experiences influenced what you believed to be true.

Memorable events such as vacations, birthdays, holiday celebrations, and the like have affected the formation of your worldview. Your first job, your first promotion, a career change — all were key learning moments that shaped your worldview. Likewise, life's tougher moments or unfortunate events have left their mark on your spirit. Your first major disagreement with a boss, a conflict with a coworker, a falling out with your spouse — each of these has a permanent influence on your life. Education, religious training, extended-family influence, participation in certain activities, and the impact of the media and its messages all mold your composite view of the world.

Your worldview does not always operate on a conscious level. In fact, it is unlikely that you are cognizant of the operation of your worldview. Many of your responses spring immediately out of your worldview without a single conscious thought. For instance, you read in the paper about a injustice done to a little child and react with sadness and disgust. That's the expression of your worldview about the tragedy of injustices done to the innocent. Your boss asks you to work through part of the weekend and you react to her request with a groan. That's your worldview about work and personal time kicking in. You're asked to donate to a particular charity and you decline. Your decision is an example of your worldview about the worthiness of the charity, or of the reality of your budget. You speed home from work, doing 80 mph on the freeway. Worldview again: breaking the speed limit is not as important as being home quickly.

Is there a gap between core principles and your worldview?

Why is it important to take a close look at your worldview? Isn't one worldview just as good as another? Aren't there different strokes for different folks?

If there are such things as core truths, we need to compare those truths to our personal worldview and then ask how closely the two align. In other words, we don't want to continue acting in accordance with a worldview that isn't aligned with the core principles of success. Right?

Now I'm not suggesting that we all adopt the same worldview. And I'm not saying there isn't room for diversity of thought and variety of expression. The challenge I'm presenting to you is this: examine your core beliefs about life — your worldview — and compare them to the core principles of truth that have been proven over time. It is only when core principles and your worldview are sufficiently aligned that you will enjoy lasting success. Without this alignment you've got what I call the "gap." Frankly, all of us have a gap. Our worldview and our behaviors don't always reflect the core principles. This is one of the major human dilemmas. We have a gap and we must determine how to close it.

It is extremely easy to read this and say "this really doesn't apply to me because I subscribe to living by core principles. This is really a message to other folks." Let me challenge you personally. This message is not for someone else. It is for you. You have a gap that needs to be closed. We all do. Your lifevision must address how you intend to close the gap. Don't be fooled into mentally agreeing with the concept of core principles while neglecting to challenge your own worldview in comparison.

Reflect on your behavior over the last day or two. It will probably be sufficient to show you where the gap exists in your life. Have all of your motives been caring and thoughtful? Were you at all selfish? Have you treated your spouse with compassion and respect, or with indifference? Have you had any run-ins with coworkers who see the world differently than you do?

The Gap

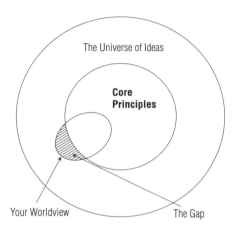

This diagram illustrates the gap. The outside circle represents a "Universe of Ideas" that includes all thoughts and concepts. This universe includes all constructs of thought and all expressions of behavior, both positive and negative, good and bad. Within the frame of the Universe of Ideas are core principles. This inner circle illustrates the fact that Core Principles are a subset of the Universe of Ideas. In other words, the larger frame includes some ideas that are core truths and some that are not. Also within the frame of the Universe of Ideas is your personal worldview. There is undoubtedly some overlap between your worldview and the core principles. But where does your worldview include the ideas, actions, and behaviors that fall outside of the core principles? Where is there a gap (illustrated by the cross-hatched region in the diagram) between the two?

Examples of behaviors in the gap include:
- Wanting to get revenge against a boss that treats you unfairly.
- Taking advantage of a trusting customer by charging a little extra.
- Embellishing your contribution to a project.
- Not telling the whole truth about a mistake where you were at least partially at fault.
- Giving your spouse the silent treatment because you're angry about they way he/she said something.
- Spreading a rumor about a coworker that you're not sure is true.
- Going behind someone's back to get what you want.

We are all guilty of behaviors in the gap. If we don't do anything to change, we are thwarting our own success in the long run. It's important to do something about closing the gap!

What can you do to close the gap?

The process of closing the gap between core principles and our worldview is not an easy process. It may take you a lifetime to get the job done, but that shouldn't dissuade you from making the conscious effort to close the gap. It is an important step toward fulfilling your lifevision.

Here are six suggested steps for closing the gap:

1. Understand your worldview.
2. Understand the core principles.
3. Admit that the gap between the two exists and define what the gap consists of.
4. Outline a specific plan to close the gap.
5. Involve your lifevision communities in assisting you with your plan.
6. Execute the plan.

Understand your worldview

One of the best ways to understand your worldview is to examine the way you spend your time, energy, and money. The basic elements of your worldview are probably best reflected by your behaviors regarding these three things.

Look at your calendar or day planner. What activities and which relationships take up the majority of your time? Take a close look at your checkbook and your credit card receipts over the course of a few months. Where, when, and how you spend your money will tell you a lot about what is important to you. Where do you spend your most passionate energy? What lights you up and gets you going? As you look at your actions in each of these categories, you should be able to put some words to your worldview.

Understand the core principles

If you thought understanding your worldview was difficult, this one is even tougher! Philosophers, theologians, scientists, business people, and millions of ordinary people like you and me have spent a lot of time searching for core truths. I spend a tremendous amount of effort trying to discover, understand, and apply core truths, and to bring my worldview into alignment with them.

Here are some practical ways to pursue a better understanding of core principles:

- *Reading great literature.* You'll discover great truths in reading the works of great authors, philosophers, and thinkers.

- *Searching the scriptures.* Whatever your religious persuasion, some of the most profound truths can be found in scripture. Take time to reflect and meditate upon these thoughtful and provoking writings.

- *Quiet reflection in natural settings.* Truth is revealed in countless ways through nature. I encourage you to spend some quiet time observing creation and the interaction of plants, animals, and the environment.

- *Prayer.* This is perhaps the most powerful tool available for the discovery of great truth. In recent Gallup surveys, it was reported that over 90 percent of Americans believe in the power of prayer. I view prayer as simply a conversation with God, seeking the revelation of truth and hope to aid me in my personal journey.

- *Formal education or training.* Take a class at the local community college. Join a book club. Attend a one-day seminar. Join a church training class. Get a degree in philosophy. There are numerous opportunities all around you. Many organizations will underwrite part of your training if it will benefit your work. I have had some of my best experiences in formal educational settings.

- *Meaningful dialogue with others.* Everyone is searching for truth and its practical application to their lives, and yet few of us take the time to talk to each other about really meaningful things. I encourage you to build relationships with others who are interested in meaningful dialogue. These discussions can occur in the workplace or a church group, in a reading club or with close personal friends. You will find the payback well worth the effort.

Admit that the gap between the two exists and define what the gap consists of

As you gain a greater understanding of core principles and your worldview, you'll be able to see the discrepancies between the two. That is, if you're honest with yourself! I've seen many people who never make it to this step. Especially in western culture, we've developed an "I'm okay, you're okay" mentality. In reality, this is a damaging thought pattern that keeps us from admitting that we have a gap and that we need to close it.

While you may, in general, succeed in aligning your behavior with principles, I challenge you to ask yourself if there are certain principles which you struggle with the most. This question will help you to pinpoint your gap. For instance, you might have difficulty telling the truth to coworkers because you're not the confrontational type. Or you may prefer to hold a grudge against a fellow employee rather than meeting with them to clear the air. You may be someone who is overly critical of things not done "your way." My biggest struggles at work are impatience with my teammates and being quick to criticize. The areas with which you struggle are also the areas where you will find the biggest discrepancy between your worldview and core principles.

Admitting that a discrepancy exists between core principles and your worldview (as well as your actions) is an important step toward closing the gap. Once you are able to see and admit the incongruity, you can move on to creating a plan of action to close the gap.

Outline a specific plan to close the gap

Here is where you integrate the concept of core principles with your lifevision! A major part of your lifevision should address how you intend to close the gap. The plan to close the gap will be unique for each person. Your plan could include any one of the following:

- Seeking out a mentor at work to give you ongoing guidance
- Setting goals in your work performance plan that have to do with closing the gap so that you can hold yourself accountable for achieving them
- Getting involved with a small group of people through a spiritual or social organization that has the specific focus of personal growth
- Regularly seeking out the counsel of your friends and coworkers in order to understand how they effectively deal with the gaps in their lives
- Setting aside a reflective time at the start of your work day so that you can focus on being a person of principle

There are many other ideas you can choose to incorporate into your lifevision plan. If you have spent an adequate amount of time on the first three steps of this process, you should have a pretty good idea of what to do.

Involve your lifevision communities in assisting you with your plan

The path to closing the gap will always be paved with help from your lifevision communities. This has been a very rewarding aspect of my search for truth and its practical application. As we're all on the same journey, it is important to tap into the insights and experiences of others. If we don't, we're making a big mistake.

The team I work with has been a big help in this regard. Both formally and informally, we've agreed to hold each other accountable for closing our own gaps. That means bringing the topic up in casual conversation as well as in team meetings. If there's a discrepancy between my actions and core principles, I give my teammates the right to challenge me. Likewise, you can establish the same kind of relationships in your work environment.

Execute the plan as part of your lifevision

This is where the real challenge — and the real fun — starts: living out your lifevision plan to close the gap. The application of principles in the context of dynamic situations and relationships is perhaps the paramount challenge of life. We won't ever get it perfect. We'll always have a new situation to confront and a new test to pass, but that's what makes life such an exciting adventure. As we seek to become people of principle in the midst of life's challenges, we will find many rewards for doing so.

Making Principled Choices in Day-to-Day Situations

As you execute your plan to close the gap, life will present you with many situations that involve a choice: a principle-centered option, and a more expedient, easier option. The consequences of your choice may be minor, or the choice you make may have a significant effect on your life. Making the principle-centered decision will probably not be easy, but you will find a stronger sense of congruence and satisfaction for having made that choice.

In your search for truth and in your efforts to close the "principle gap," you will periodically end up pitting "right" versus "wrong." Although it may be difficult to make the right choice due to the personal cost involved, you know that the long-term payoff will be there. Enduring the short-term pain may seem difficult or discouraging. This is what Scott Peck tells us in his best seller *The Road Less Traveled*. We will be tempted to take the easier road, avoiding short-term pain, instead of the narrow road that involves confronting the principle challenge head on. The greater your awareness of principles, however, the more natural it will become to make the right choices. As you practice making principled choices you'll discover the benefits outweigh any short-term discomfort.

Let me illustrate with a story from my own career. By the early 1990's, I had experienced rapid career advancement. Promoted to partner in a national CPA firm by age 30, I enjoyed widespread respect throughout my office, with one major exception. I'll call him Walt.

Walt, a fellow partner, worked in a different area of the firm, and therefore our paths rarely crossed. However, we began to have a series of run-ins. We took turns giving each other negative performance reviews based on what each of us believed to be an accurate perception of the other. It got to the point that I believed Walt's comments about me to other partners were less than accurate. I had never faced such a situation in my entire career. I had always been able to work things out with coworkers. Walt persisted with his negative view of the way I approached my work.

Instead of getting back at Walt or letting the situation reach a boiling point, I sought him out for a meeting to clear the air. I gained a fair amount of insight into Walt's view of me and my department. I realized he had some valid points. Perhaps in my enthusiasm to run a people-centered department, I had disenfranchised other departments. I had created some barriers between my team and the other teams in the office. Some of Walt's perceptions about me were flat wrong, of course. My basic motivation was not to build a "fiefdom," as he claimed, nor to carry myself about the office as a prima donna. Yet those were Walt's perceptions of my behavior. Although the session was uncomfortable for both of us, I believe it eased some of the tension between us. Though we never became best friends, I do think our discussion helped us to respect each other.

It would have been much easier for me to continue the struggle with Walt. The more difficult choice was to attempt to work the situation out, honoring the principle of respecting each other and working together for a mutually beneficial outcome. Although the discussion was awkward, the long-term payoff was worth the discomfort.

Of course, I can't claim to make the principled choice all the time. But my level of awareness has been raised to the point where I am able to diagnose situations that call for it. As your own awareness increases, you'll find a new perspective on tough decisions, inside and outside of work.

Right v. Right

We'll always have "right" versus "wrong" situations to deal with. How about "right" versus "right," when one principle, or truth, collides with another? These can be exasperating situations.

You might find yourself in a situation where one of your coworkers, with whom you're good friends, is engaging in dishonest behavior that is costing your company money. The principles of loyalty and respect for your friend have collided with the principles of honoring your employer and being truthful. You may have a situation where your company has a policy that a particular customer seems to be taking advantage of. Do you allow the customer to have his way, or do you confront that customer? What about the employee who really does a great job but can't get along with her fellow workers? Is it right to retain her because she gets the job done, or should she be let go? As you can see from these examples, there aren't any easy answers when principles run into each other.

This is what makes our commitment to wrestle with principles — to understand them, to apply them to our lives, to examine the gaps in our behavior — so important. If we're not constantly engaged in this wrestling as part of the discovery and alignment of our lifevision, then we are not growing and maturing as we should be. In order to fulfill your lifevision in the most capable and effective manner, you must be constantly engaged in the pursuit of becoming a person of principle.

Concluding Thoughts on Becoming a Person of Principle

Becoming a person of principle is one of the important lessons I learned from my father. I saw him face many dilemmas and wrestle with the real world application of principles. Rarely were those situations easy. Whether it involved losing money on a landscaping contract in order to please a customer or giving to someone in need when there were plenty of needs in our own family, my father struggled with his decisions. Did he always make the right choice? I'm sure he would tell you that he didn't. But by his example, I learned that the discovery and fulfillment of our life purpose is integrally linked to discovering, wrestling with, and applying truth to our lives.

Who in your life sets an inspiring example? Who is mentoring you on becoming a person of character? I encourage you to build relationships with those in your lifevision communities who can guide you in this endeavor.

Chapter 3 Tool Kit

Exercise 3-1: *Your Time, Energy, and Money*

One of the best ways to evaluate your worldview is to examine where you're spending your time, energy, and money. Use the following exercise to evaluate your priorities.

Question	Time	Energy	Money
Where are you spending the largest or most consistent amounts of each of these areas?			
What do your "spending patterns" in each of these areas tell you about your worldview?			
Is there anything you need to change as a result of looking at your behaviors in each of these areas?			

Exercise 3-2: Defining Your Values

Another way to look at worldview is to define your values. Use this worksheet to define what is most important to you.

1. What are your most basic values? You can use the list below to help, or add your own.

Happiness	Absence of conflict	Creativity
Security	Physical fitness	Innovation
Significance	Spiritual maturity	Questioning
Wealth	Friends	Searching
Health	Making a differ-	Dominating
Family	ence	Succeeding
Relationships	Excellence	Recognition
Inner peace	Improvement	Fame
Balance	Worship	Vision
Working hard	Inner reflection	Reverence
Leisure	Meaningful work	Challenge
Competition	Progress	Influencing
Winning	Integrity	Accomplishing
Giving	Leading	Leaving a legacy
	Following	

2. What are your most important priorities right now?

3. What are the character attributes that you would like to express in your attitudes, words, and actions?

Chapter 3 Tool Kit

Exercise 3-3: *Activities to Understand Your Worldview Better*

This chapter presented several ideas for better understanding your worldview. Complete the following table.

Activity	Do you do this now? Why or why not?	What do you think the value of this activity is? Why?	Is this activity something you should consider? If so, how should you go about it?
Great literature			
Scripture			
Reflection on nature			
Prayer			
Formal education			
Meaningful dialogue			

Part II

Aligning Your Lifevision and Your Work

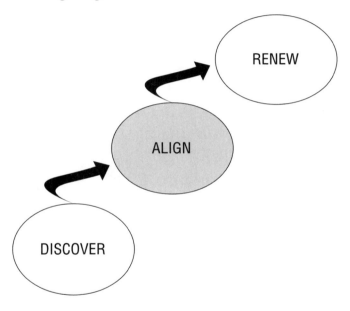

Chapter 4

Your Company and Alignment
Corporate Strategies for Achieving Alignment

"We're trying to create an environment for our employees so that they can find the fulfillment they are looking for in their lives through their work here and a congruence between the corporation's objectives and their objectives."

> —Bill George, CEO of Medtronic,
> Winner of Business Ethics Award
> for General Excellence in Ethics

Pick up any business periodical today and you don't have to read very far to conclude that the business environment of the late nineties is vastly different than that of the seventies, eighties or even the early nineties. The amount of change over the last three decades has been breathtaking. The rules of the game have changed. Command and control are out. Participation and empowerment are in. A singular focus on quality products has been supplanted by a shift toward complete value packages which include quality product, timely delivery, and superior service at a reasonable cost. Constant change has replaced stability and security. Past successes guarantee nothing about the future. As Dorothy said to Toto, "I don't think we're in Kansas anymore."

The amount and frequency of change in today's marketplace is alarming. New technologies, globalization, razor-sharp competition, demanding consumers, and increasingly mobile employees are all part of the collage of change. You don't need to look very far for examples of companies that have suffered because of this changing marketplace. Many companies acclaimed as "the best of the best" in the popular management book *In Search of Excellence* have either disappeared or are very different from when they were profiled only a short time ago.

We are presently in one of the most profound eras of marketplace restructuring, repositioning, and realigning. The changes that we have become so accustomed to will continue, both in quantity and pace. Industry shakeouts will continue. Employees will build their résumés in order to become more marketable. Customers will have more choices and will demand higher quality for a lower price. Battles will intensify as the stakes get higher.

Changing Times Require Changing Thinking	
THEN	**NOW**
Working Harder	Working Smarter
Command & Control	Empowerment
Stability & Security	Constant Change
Managing	Leading
Satisfy the Customer	Exceed Customer Expectations
Provide Jobs for Employees	Offer Employees Meaning and Fulfillment
Quality = Excellent Product,	Quality = Excellent Product Timely Delivery, & Superior Service
The Future is an Extension of the Past	Paradigm Changes Result in Discontinuous Future
Information is a Good Thing to Have	Information is a Competitive Weapon

The robust economy of the last decade or so has given many executives the false assurance that the future will merely be an extension of the past. Nothing could be further from the truth. Robert Reich, former Secretary of Labor, says, "Now is the most dangerous time, because we don't see the pressure building. But the heat is being turned up. The terms of competition are changing dramatically." Reich believes that the prosperous state of the economy is lulling U.S. businesses into a false sense of security.

To paraphrase the futurist Joel Barker, probably the only thing we can count on about the future is that it will be discontinuous and different from the present. In other words, the future will not be a continuation of the past. He has shared this concept with us through his excellent work in the area of paradigms. Through the phenomenon of paradigm shift — which seems to be happening at an ever increasing pace in the last ten years — we can be guaranteed that the future will look quite different than today.

What is your company doing to prepare for a discontinuous future? How is it arming itself against well-capitalized and information-rich competitors? What is it doing to develop new methodologies for delivering products and services at higher quality and lower cost? **Most importantly, what is your company doing to ensure alignment of its people with its purpose?** In this chapter, I'll explore the phenomenon of alignment from a corporate point of view. I'll discuss the necessity for alignment and address the corporate-level strategies that can make it happen.

Why start here? Isn't this a book about what you can personally do to achieve alignment? Yes. And your first steps toward alignment with your company start with an awareness of what elements are necessary for alignment to occur. You can then assess what stage your company is at, where your company is going, and how likely it is that they will take the appropriate steps toward alignment.

The Knowledge Age and Alignment

Peter Drucker has told us that business has moved full throttle into the Knowledge Age. We have moved from an agrarian- to an industrial- to an information-based economy. Information, and the applied knowledge extracted from that information, now defines competitive advantage. This economy is much more about what you know than the tangible assets you own.

Today the majority of the workforce is engaged in knowledge or service sector work. In 1920, there were over 11.5 million farm workers compared to less than 900,000 today. Railroads employed over 2,000,000 workers after the turn of the century compared to less than 250,000 today. Today's workforce employs well over a million computer programmers and almost two million engineers. New industries have arisen throughout this knowledge revolution. In a recent employment projection in Illinois for the year 2005, eleven of the top twelve positions were in the service and knowledge sectors. Well over three million knowledge and service jobs, ranging from marketing and sales to teaching and library sciences, are projected in these 11 categories.

What's so important about this huge shift in how America works? In the middle of the information age, Tom Peters tells us that knowledge workers are busy "building their résumés." They are acquiring key skills and capabilities which transfer to other environments. Drucker also tells us that knowledge workers are looking for meaning and fulfillment in their work. They want to align themselves with companies that have both a well-defined purpose and a method for aligning their employees with that purpose. If an employer is not facilitating alignment, a knowledge worker will look for another opportunity.

A recent survey of 55,000 workers, conducted by the Gallup organization and reported in the January 12, 1998 issue of *Fortune*, documents the importance of alignment. The poll determined that the following four employee beliefs correlated with better financial results for companies:

- **workers feel they are given the opportunity to do what they do best every day**
- **they believe their opinions count**
- **they sense that their fellow workers are committed to quality**

- **they've made a direct connection between their work and the company's mission**

Alignment is far from simply an academic concept or the latest management trend. It is a real-world practice employed by the best of today's high performance companies. The best companies understand the revolution that is occurring in business today. They know that people are indeed their most important resource. They are taking real action to ensure that employees are finding meaning and fulfillment in their work. And these companies are being paid handsomely in return.

Why are we seeing such significant results from alignment? Alignment eliminates waste. Period. If people understand the purpose of the company, understand their own purpose within that company, and see how the two fit together, misunderstandings and miscommunications decrease. Alignment takes people to previously unattained levels of performance. They begin to discover capabilities, attitudes, and skills which were dormant before, and their performance most assuredly increases. When alignment is happening, employees remain faithful to companies and costly turnover is reduced. There are many other reasons, but these are some of the most significant. I'm confident that as the economy of the United States becomes even more knowledge-based, alignment will become more than just a good idea — it will be absolutely essential for survival.

Lifevision Diagram 4: *Your Company and Alignment*

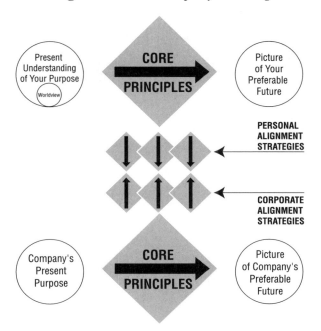

Principle: *In times of change, alignment is not just a good idea, but a competitive necessity.*

Paradox: *Making alignment happen requires the collaborative efforts of all — leaders and employees alike.*

Just like you have a personal purpose that is moving forward toward your vision of a preferable future, your company has a purpose and is also moving toward its vision. Many business books have been written about corporate purpose, mission, and vision, but we have failed to understand the relationship between our personal lifevision and that of our companies.

Just like you are moving forward in time toward a point on the horizon, your company is making progress towards the "picture of its preferable future." Many organizations call this their vision statement, describing a specific state that they wish to achieve. And just like people, companies are governed by an operative set of core principles — the same core principles as those in Diagram 3.

Diagram 4 shows the juxtaposition of personal purpose and your company's purpose. The vertical arrows represent the efforts that both you and your company must make in order to achieve alignment with one another. (The arrows pointing up illustrate corporate alignment strategies. The arrows pointing down represent personal alignment strategies). These efforts will bring your purposes closer together and keep them moving in the same direction.

Before discussing personal alignment strategies, this chapter focuses on corporate-level strategies for alignment. Here is why:

- Awareness of company strategies will allow you to appreciate the difficulty of achieving alignment from a leader's viewpoint. In a sense, you'll get to walk in your leaders' shoes for a bit.

- As your understanding of corporate strategies increases, you can begin to assess your own company and see how it measures up. Is it supporting alignment through its practical day-to-day actions? How?

- You need to assess your own sphere of influence in the company. Can you support the corporate strategies for achieving alignment? Better yet, can you take the initiative in making some of them happen?

- Finally, you must assess whether you, your company, and its leaders can make the efforts required to improve alignment in the future.

**Understanding Corporate Strategies
for Achieving Alignment**

As you seek to achieve alignment between your personal life-vision and your company's purpose, it's important to understand what companies are doing to support alignment and just how difficult the process can be. Organizational efforts at alignment can be grouped into three categories: **strategic, operational, and cultural**. There are many potential actions for companies to consider in each of these three categories. However, there are a few strategies essential to all attempts at alignment, outlined below.

Key Strategic Action Steps for Alignment

- Developing a well-defined corporate purpose, including mission, vision, and values

- Designing a corporate purpose and strategy that consciously values, empowers, and rewards people

- Repeatedly communicating the corporate purpose in multiple venues

- Openly sharing information about the company's progress toward achieving it's purpose with employees

Key Operational Action Steps for Alignment

- Matching employees' skills and experience to the

right positions, then allowing them to meet the position's demands in a creative manner

- Implementing measurement and accountability systems that encourage employees to act in accordance with the corporate purpose and strategic direction

- Rewarding high performance that is in alignment with the company's goals

- Eliminating all systems and procedures which are counterproductive to the alignment process

Key Cultural Action Steps for Alignment
- Storytelling that simultaneously renews the value of people and the purpose of the organization

- Offering employee training that supports the discovery and alignment of personal lifevision

- Creating an open learning environment where employee participation in decision making is encouraged

- Walking the talk of alignment!

Key Strategic Action Steps for Alignment
The strategic level is the highest organizational level, as it concerns the overall purpose and direction of the company. It is

therefore the most critical level at which alignment is embraced. If it isn't happening here, it won't make much difference at the operational or cultural levels. The following four actions are each strategic in nature. They have to do with alignment in its most foundational form.

Developing a well-defined corporate purpose, including mission, vision, and values

It's surprising how many middle market organizations have not taken the time to define their corporate mission, vision, and values. Yet this is a key step in becoming a high performance organization in which there is alignment. Why? Because in the absence of clear definitions, employees, customers, shareholders, and suppliers will draw their own conclusions based on personal interpretations. Multiple interpretations lead to lack of alignment. If companies want each of these groups singing from the same sheet of music, then it makes sense to start with a clear definition of the corporate purpose.

In my work with hundreds of middle-market organizations, one of the most consistent themes I hear from employees is that they don't really understand where the company is headed or what its top priorities are. Leaders often take it for granted that employees and customers understand the corporate mission, vision, and values, when in fact they do not. Therefore, it makes sense to clearly define why the company exists, where it is headed, and what its priorities are. All high-performance companies take the time to examine these questions, work through the answers, and develop well articulated statements of purpose.

The Three Basic Elements of Corporate Purpose:

Mission: Answers a few key questions, including "Why does the organization exist?", "Who are its customers?" and "What are the customers' needs?" It defines the essence of why the organization opens its doors and stays in business.

Vision: A clear picture of what the organization hopes to become by some specific point in the future. Put another way, the vision is where the organization hopes to end up if it can faithfully execute its mission.

Values: The core ideology to which the organization is committed; the "code of behavior" it subscribes to as it does business. Values will, in all likelihood, be based on the core principles we discussed in Chapter 3.

Your challenge is to discover each of these elements within your organization. If you happen to have the good fortune of working for a company that has already articulated its purpose, then your job should be pretty easy. If not, I recommend that you take an informal survey of sorts. Talk to a few key customers, a sampling of employees, and some of the leaders in the organization. Ask the following questions:

- Why is this business in business?
- Who are our customers?
- What are our customers' needs?
- What will the company look like in five years?
- What about what we hope to become looks different from today's organization?
- What seems to be the "code of behavior" that we subscribe to in our dealings with customers and with each other?

If the answers to your survey are largely inconsistent, this may be a symptom of deeper problems within the organization. I have worked with organizations where this is the case. They seem to have an organizational schizophrenia, unsure of who they are or where they are headed. Attempting to align with something that is so unfocused is difficult.

Hopefully you'll find a degree of consistency with your survey, and you'll be able to discover your organization's mission, vision, and values.

Designing a corporate purpose and strategy that consciously values, empowers, and rewards people

Companies that adopt an overall strategy of valuing, empowering, and rewarding people have found that the payback is awesome. The increasingly competitive nature of the business environment calls for some radically new approaches to valuing people, tapping into their potential, and aligning their purpose with that of the organization. We are heading into uncharted territory in the decade ahead. We need to toss out dated approaches to "managing people" and learn how to truly serve them and help them prosper. In return, our organizations will be paid back with exceptional performance. As you stand back and assess the situation, how would you say your company rates on valuing and serving its employees?

An article in the December 28, 1997 *Chicago Tribune* illustrates this point:

"Today, much has changed, say employment experts. Finding themselves in a far more competitive market for topnotch workers, American companies are putting on a more human face.

Many employers are initiating programs to encourage lateral movement and mentoring that help employees develop new skills and enhance current ones. And a few of the more progressive companies are even taking on the challenge of helping their people gain a better grip on the delicate balance between life and career."

So what are some of the progressive companies doing? Take a look at Southwest Airlines, which *Fortune* magazine recently ranked as the number one company to work for in America. Southwest's practical actions toward valuing their employees are world-renowned. In fact, they're known as the company where customers are number two and employees are number one. If you visit their corporate headquarters, you'll be greeted by a massive sign that proclaims:

"The people of Southwest Airlines are 'the creators' of what we have become — and of what we will be.

Our people transformed an idea into a legend. That legend will continue to grow only so long as it is nourished — by our people's indomitable spirit, boundless energy, immense goodwill, and burning desire to excel.

Our thanks — and our love — to the people of Southwest Airlines for creating a marvelous family and a wondrous airline!"

What's this? A company talking about love? In the book *Nuts! Southwest Airlines' Crazy Recipe for Business and Personal Success*, the authors document how this remarkable company backs up its talk. Employee ownership, times of celebration, constant communication, and employee recognition awards are all practical expressions of Southwest's culture of serving their people. This radical culture of affirmation and love has produced some of the best results in the airline industry.

Another example is Hewlett-Packard. This company, founded decades ago, has wavered little from its original core values. In so doing, it has become one of the greatest success stories in American industry, surviving and thriving in the midst of one of the fastest-changing industries on the planet. One of H-P's core values is honoring and valuing employees. They take extraordinary steps to ensure that their people are some of the happiest and most well-aligned employees around. Examples of the practical ways that H-P values its people include providing state-of-the-art working facilities, a benefits package that puts most other companies to shame, and a regular distribution of corporate profits to all employees. That's what I call putting your money where your mouth is!

Frankly, we need a whole lot more than just a few "progressive" companies working at this level. My question for business leaders everywhere is this: what are you doing to make your organization one that focuses on its purpose through valuing and serving your employees? Even if you're not in a leadership position, you do have a sphere of influence in your organization. How can you make a difference by valuing, serving, and empowering others?

Repeatedly communicating the corporate purpose in multiple venues

There can never be enough communication regarding the corporate mission, vision, and values. Because business is complex and each day presents a new twist on implementing the company's strategy, communication is an absolute must. How is your company doing in this area? Is communication plentiful and informative, or is it sparse and rather useless? Are leaders taking the initiative to communicate? Are you?

Here is where a grass roots effort can pay off. I have worked with a number of companies where someone other than a leader initiated a newsletter or some other forum of communication. One of my clients in Portland, Talbot, Korvola & Warwick, LLP, does an excellent job of using their newsletter to promote the company's mission, vision, and values. Each month, the newsletter shares a practical story about living out the company's purpose. Readers are inspired by seeing the company's mission in action. Through the regular use of a simple communication tool, this organization is perpetuating its purpose. The newsletter isn't coordinated by the company leaders. It's a true grass roots effort!

If you are in a position of leadership or influence, communication of the corporate purpose and related goals needs to be frequent, and both formal and informal. Over-communicating is a more forgivable error than the opposite.

If you aren't in a leadership position, consider what you can do to facilitate communication about the company purpose. Perhaps you can focus on increasing communication about the purpose of your department or team. These small efforts, team by team and department by department, can have a great cumulative impact.

Openly sharing information about the company's
progress toward achieving its purpose with employees

The command and control mindset of the industrial era is just about dead. This is the Information Age. Many companies have realized that the open sharing of information with employees helps workers make better decisions.

This concept has been popularized under the name open book management. Employees are provided with information about the company's progress toward achieving its purpose, and are shown how their individual efforts fit into the bigger picture. As employees understand how their job fits into the overall purpose of the organization, they take a big step forward in becoming better aligned.

Key Operational Action Steps for Alignment

The second arena where alignment can be actively encouraged is at the operational level — the day-to-day procedures and systems that the company uses to get things done. Each organization has systems that can be used to facilitate and strengthen alignment, moving it from the strategic, conceptual level to the practical, everyday level. The following four action steps are among the most basic that a company can take as it strives for alignment.

Matching employees' skills and experience to the right
positions, then allowing them to meet the position's
demands in a creative manner

Employees today bring a variety of skills and experiences to their positions. They are more educated and more highly trained than any group of people in the history of business. This is one of the telling characteristics of the Information Age, and it's because of this fact that companies are getting much more creative in their approach to job descriptions. They're throwing out rigid and constraining definitions of how a particular position is supposed to function. In place of these highly structured (and hence outdated) position descriptions, companies are allowing more room for creative expression and maximum utilization of their people's talents.

I know that most of you want to use all of your "head, hands, and heart" in your work. You want the opportunity to express your individuality through your work and to give it your all. That's difficult to do when a work position is narrowly defined or heavily structured. Many of today's progressive companies are in the middle of creating more flexible positions that take advantage of what employees have to offer. They help employees take stock of their specific skills, talents, and abilities, and then match people to the right positions.

One of my clients in San Diego is doing a great job in this area. RD Instruments is a small manufacturer of high-tech scientific equipment. Central to their mission are these words: "RDI is a growing, profitable enterprise where people earn a living while enjoying a meaningful and rewarding experience." These are more than just words. I've had the privilege of working with them for over a year, and when it comes to valuing and empowering their people, they live this mission. They do it primarily through job descriptions that have a lot of creative freedom and by matching people to where they fit best. Each employee is encouraged to accomplish their job in a way that's interesting and meaningful. As employees have grown and developed over time, this approach has resulted in a lot of promotion from within. It's obvious that people enjoy working there, and that many are experiencing alignment!

Implementing measurement and accountability systems that encourage employees to act in accordance with the corporate purpose and strategic direction

One of the top reasons companies fail to experience the results they desire is failure to implement systems that measure performance and hold people accountable to the plan. Most middle market organizations get caught up in the day-to-day fire fighting, while ignoring proper measurement and accountability systems that would extinguish most fires in the first place.

Accountability systems are good for everyone, though employees sometimes treat them like nasty medicine that they've been forced to swallow. This usually happens when the systems are poorly designed or communicated. If established and explained properly, these systems can reinforce behavior that is in alignment with the company's goals while directly affirming employee successes.

Rewarding high performance that is in alignment with the company's goals

Employees need to be rewarded, both financially and in other ways, in order to achieve full alignment with the company. One of the most important elements of a measurement and accountability system is the reward component. Employee performance that meets or exceeds planned targets should be properly rewarded. This is a simple concept that many companies constantly wrestle with.

In employee surveys conducted by our firm, failure to have the proper reward systems in place consistently ranks as a problem area. The difficulty, of course, is designing the appropriate mix of tangible and intangible rewards that meets the needs of a diverse employee population. If well designed and implemented, the right forms of compensation and rewards will go a long way toward producing alignment.

Last year, I completed a consultation with a middle market construction company located in Silicon Valley. Here is a company that is experiencing rapid growth and excellent profits in one of the country's hottest business environments. A well designed corporate reward system is part of their plan.

One of the first things I did when engaged to work for this company was interview each of the members of the senior leadership team. These guys genuinely enjoyed working for Air Systems and were proud of what they'd accomplished. A common theme of the interviews was the company's commitment to a core set of values, treating people with respect and honoring the customer.

I also discovered their intensive commitment to their people. How did they demonstrate this? First, through an attitude of caring and listening. But they went much farther than that. Air Systems is committed to having their people participate in decision making by using a servant-leader model with the entire management team. Further, Air Systems is committed to open sharing of financial information with all of its people. They figure that people ought to know what's going on!

Maybe the most tangible evidence of its commitment to people is in the form of a novel gainsharing program. In the last several years, Air Systems has shared with all of its employees, on a quarterly basis, a significant portion of its profit. Talk about motivation. This company constantly challenges its people to think about why the company is in business and what their respective roles are in helping the company meet its goals. As those goals are met, the company rewards employees with a healthy financial bonus.

Eliminating all systems and procedures which are counterproductive to the alignment process

Strange as it may seem, many organizations have systems and procedures in place today simply because "that's the way it's always been done." In today's fast-changing, increasingly competitive environment, this posture is disastrous — especially if the systems get in the way of alignment.

Common examples of systems that inhibit alignment include:
- compensation and promotion systems that reward longevity before performance
- outdated communication systems
- policies that keep employees in the dark about the company's direction and performance
- human resource departments that resemble paper-shuffling personnel bureaus rather than proactive employee-serving forces
- bureaucracies and antiquated procedures that increase the amount of time it takes to complete simple tasks

I encourage you to examine the systems and procedures in your area of focus and ask a simple question: "Is this procedure helping or hindering the alignment of our people?" Once you answer that question, you can begin the process of dismantling and replacing dysfunctional procedures with those that promote alignment. Again, this is an area where all employees can get in on the act. Most companies I've worked with appreciate employee suggestions about streamlining and improvement. Some companies even offer financial incentives for suggestions that increase efficiency or that end up saving the company money.

Key Cultural Action Steps for Alignment

The third arena of alignment concerns the organization's culture, the human side of how things are done. Culture concerns how people work together, how they communicate, how leaders interact with employees, how customers are treated, and so forth. If alignment is embraced at the strategic and operational levels, but essentially discouraged in the company's everyday culture, it will die off quickly. The culture must support alignment. The following are four cultural action steps companies can take to ensure that alignment is kept alive and well.

Storytelling that simultaneously renews the value
of people and the purpose of the organization

Storytelling is one of the real power tools that leaders can employ to perpetuate the company's mission, vision, and values. Storytelling is about renewing each employee's commitment to the corporate purpose and direction, and honoring them in the achievement of their personal goals. I like the way Max DePree, in his book *Leadership is An Art*, explains the importance of leaders (what he calls "tribal elders") as storytellers:

"Tribal storytellers, the tribe's elders, must insistently

work at the process of corporate renewal. They must preserve and revitalize the values of the tribe. They nourish a scrutiny of corporate values that eradicates bureaucracy and sustains the individual. Constant renewal also readies us for the inevitable crises of corporate life. The goal of renewal is to be a corporate entity that gives us space to reach our potential as individuals and, through that, as a corporation. Renewal comes through genuine service to others. It cannot come about through a process of mere self-perpetuation. Renewal is an outward orientation of service, rather than an inward orientation of maintenance. Renewal is the concern of everyone, but is the special province of the tribal storyteller."

Yes, storytelling is the special province of the leaders. They are the ones we look up to and from whom we draw our inspiration. But have you checked your own communication skills lately? The truth is, we can all be storytellers. We can make the choice to positively communicate our company's, our team's, or our department's purpose. Is your communication perpetuating the organizational or team goals?

Offering employee training that supports the discovery and alignment of personal lifevision

Many companies are recognizing the importance of work-life balance and alignment by offering training workshops in a variety of topics. As the *Chicago Tribune* article pointed out, this is a relatively new area and solutions are still being developed. Offering workshop settings for employees can help them discover and align their personal lifevision with the organization. Peter Drucker tells us that knowledge workers are seeking fulfillment and alignment with the right organization, and they'll seek other employment if the company isn't facilitating it.

In designing and supporting alignment training workshops, companies must recognize that there are always two levels of change occurring simultaneously: personal and organizational. Most corporate training and education (and most corporate improvement, for that matter) has to do with the organizational level of change. In the process, personal change is often ignored. Yet it is this change that really drives the success of organizational change. It is what makes or breaks alignment. People need to be equipped to understand organizational change, and they need to believe in and support it. If they don't, it won't work. This is probably one of the key reasons total quality management, reengineering programs, and similar corporate improvement initiatives typically experience failure rates of 75 percent or greater. These initiatives are essentially focused on work processes and procedures, with little attention paid to the human or personal aspects of change. Companies seeking to align employees with corporate purpose must address the personal aspect of change. It is at this most basic level that real change takes place.

Let me give an example. Our own organization has been piloting a major change initiative known as the Strategic Improvement Process, or SIP. The focus of SIP, as it's name implies, has been the re-engineering of selected corporate processes in order to become more efficient and to increase bottom-line performance.

Where have we found the most difficulty in executing the directives of SIP? You guessed it—in the human, or cultural, level. We've discovered that our processes certainly need fixing, and that we can redesign a process to make it work more efficiently. It has been an even greater challenge to help people understand why a process needs to be changed, what their role in new process will be, and how they can adapt their past behaviors to the "new way of doing things." It's far from a clean and easy process. People don't like to change, and old institutional habits die hard. Our organization has invested a great deal of time and money in helping people with the cultural side of change. In fact, the hard dollars spent on consultants and process changes probably pale in comparison to the "soft dollars" we've spent on personal change.

Diagnosing a problem and designing a solution to fix the problem is the easy part. The difficulty comes in implementing the solution. People don't understand the new solution. They feel threatened by it. They don't want to modify old ways of doing things. Some try to sabotage the change; others openly resist it. Yes, change is possible, but it takes a lot of effort. There must be a commitment to openness and participation, and people must be given the right tools to manage and deal with the change. That's why I recommend training workshops that are specifically designed with these facts in mind.

Creating an open learning environment where employee participation in decision making is encouraged

Employees want to participate. They want to learn. They want to share their ideas and to be able to take appropriate risks. In the past, employees were often unable to express their creativity or share their ideas in the workplace. Today, most organizations realize that their people want to actively participate in making decisions and are eager to learn new skills.

Leaders need to establish an environment that encourages the participation and input of employees. They must create a true learning environment, as Peter Senge tells us in *The Fifth Discipline*. In such an environment, people are prompted to take appropriate risks and to challenge the system. They aren't punished for trying something new or making a mistake. As risks are taken and new ideas are tested, the company will discover a more effective way to fulfill its purpose. In turn, the organization will be rewarded by employees who feel more aligned and who are an active, successful part of the organization.

Walking the talk of alignment!

Finally, and perhaps most importantly of all, we must all walk the talk of alignment. This is especially true of organizational leaders. There is no better stimulus for employees than a servant leader who models the way of alignment.

As such, leaders must define their own lifevisions and bring them into active alignment with the organization. They must be diligent about it. Those that make this commitment will give others the same enthusiasm for alignment.

Let me illustrate the principle of walking the talk of alignment. I recently took up running — at age 35. I had been talking about it for years, but had never started an exercise program. The reality of the situation was that my walk was not consistent with my talk. That's a problem that a lot of companies and a lot of people seem to have these days.

Many companies are well intentioned, but they often do little more than talk about valuing employees. If company leaders do not make the commitment to personal alignment, they will find it very difficult to encourage alignment in others. The most successful companies have leaders that relentlessly seek to align their everyday behaviors with the overall corporate purpose. Not too long ago I worked with a company where the chief executive believed that his job could be summed up in three simple directives: (1) value our employees, (2) adhere to our core values in all that we do, and (3) align all strategies with the overall corporate purpose. Simple enough.

Concluding Thoughts on Your Company

What about your organization? Is it walking the talk of alignment? Do the day to day actions of the company executives and key decision makers reflect the organization's purpose? Do employees support the purpose and help to move the company forward toward its vision? Are the strategies being executed by the company consistent with each other and with the overall mission?

You probably don't have to look too hard to answer the above questions. A scientific study isn't needed, nor is a statistically valid survey. Casual observation for about a week's time is all it takes. Look around. How are your coworkers behaving? What are the key leaders devoting their time and energy to? How are customers being served? Is there a strong commitment to a common set of goals?

I would hope that the answers to the above questions will reassure you that your organization is committed to its stated purpose and is bringing employees into alignment with that purpose. If not, you need to ask a few more questions. Is your organization likely to move toward alignment? Can you exert some positive influence in this regard, or is there little hope of positive change? Your honest assessment of the situation will help you to decide whether or not to stay with the company and become a voice for change, or to join another organization that is working toward alignment.

The primary objective of the framework presented in this chapter is to raise your level of awareness of the complicated task that your company faces. Alignment is difficult. While companies are learning more about alignment and trying out selected strategies, we still have a lot to learn about how alignment really works. Be patient with your company. Do your best to understand it and where it's coming from. Give your leaders the benefit of the doubt in improving alignment in the future. Finally, assess your own level of influence within the organization. What can you do at the corporate level to increase alignment for yourself and others?

Chapter 4 Tool Kit

Exercise 4-1: *Assessing Your Company*

The following list includes several actions that high performance companies use to increase alignment and experience better operating results. Use it to evaluate how your company is doing by scoring each item from 1 (low) to 5 (high). The assessment should give you an overall idea where your company stands and help you discern its ability to adapt and change in the future.

Purpose

_____ The organization has a clearly articulated mission and vision.

_____ Employees understand the organizational purpose and their role in fulfilling it.

_____ Organizational strategies directly support the organizational purpose.

_____ Customer input is regularly gathered to assess whether the organization is meeting customer needs.

_____ The organization's customers know what the organizational purpose is.

_____ Business processes and practices are continuously examined with an end goal of improving value and service to customers.

_____ The company attempts to eliminate all systems and procedures which are counterproductive to the alignment process.

_____ Storytelling is used to promote the organizational purpose and personal alignment with that purpose.

_____ The organization regularly celebrates successes.

_____ The organizational goals between departments and functions are well coordinated.

People

_____ Information is shared openly with employees.

_____ The company believes it is important for people to find meaning and fulfillment in their work.

_____ Active participation and input of employees in decision making is encouraged.

_____ Accountability and measurement systems are in place to accurately gauge employees' alignment with organizational goals.

_____ Employees share directly in the profitable performance of the organization.

_____ Employees are offered training opportunities to dis cover and align their lifevision.

_____ Employees are rewarded in relation to their perform ance.

_____ The organization facilitates "ownership" of organizational goals by employees.

_____ The organization truly values and respects its people.

_____ Employees are encouraged to work together to accomplish organizational goals.

Principles

_____ The organization has clearly articulated values.

_____ The leaders and managers in the organization "walk their talk."

_____ Training is provided for making ethical, principle-centered business decisions.

_____ The organization facilitates an inspiring, motivational culture.

_____ The organization encourages continuous learning among all employees.

_____ The organization believes that change is a necessary ingredient for progress.

_____ People are allowed to try new ideas without fear of failure.

_____ The organization encourages creative approaches to problem solving.

_____ People are proud to work for the organization.

Exercise 4-2: *Assessing Your Organizational Sphere of Influence*

Understanding your sphere of influence within your organization is important. Knowing the extent of your influence and the strength of your interpersonal relationships will give you a foundation for making positive change happen in your company. Answer each of the questions below.

1. Describe your current position in the company. What are your primary responsibilities?

2. Detail your history with the organization. What steps have you taken to get to your current position?

3. Who reports to you? How would you describe the quality of the relationship you have with your direct reports? In particular, describe the nature of your influence on them.

4. Who do you report to? How would you describe the quality of the relationship you have with your boss(es) or supervisor(s)? In particular, describe the nature of your influence on them.

5. Who do you consider your organizational peers? How would you describe the quality of these rela-

tionships? In particular, describe the nature of your influence on them.

6. Do you have other informal relationships in the organization in which you exercise particular influence?

7. As you contemplate ways to make positive change in your company, list the top three areas which you could influence.

Chapter 5

You and Alignment
Personal Strategies for Achieving Alignment

"Do not wait for leaders. Do it alone. Person-to-person."
—Mother Teresa of Calcutta

While alignment starts with an understanding of corporate-level strategies, most of the power to make it happen rests at the personal level. That means each employee must make a decision to align and then take the necessary steps to make it happen. As you make the personal decision to discover your lifevision and align it with your company, you're taking one of the most important steps toward improving your work performance. At the same time, your company will experience the benefits of your increased performance and the two of you can create a positive, upward spiral of continuous improvement in both performance and results.

Alignment shouldn't be confused with "company man" clichés or 1950's black-and-white educational films in which employees are told to behave like everyone else. Alignment doesn't mean becoming a corporate automaton; it means making the lifevision community of You and Your Work rich and satisfying. In the end, everyone wins.

Lifevision Diagram 5: *You and Alignment*

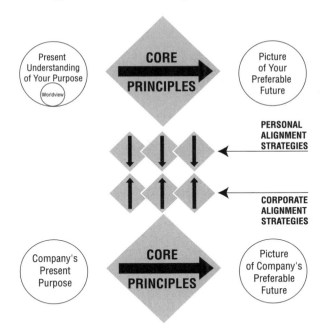

Principle: *You, not your company, hold the position of power in making alignment happen.*

Paradox: *Alignment in the past is no guarantee of alignment in the future!*

This illustration is the same as the diagram from Chapter 4, but in this chapter I'll focus on personal strategies for achieving alignment. Corporate-level strategies alone are not enough; individual actions are vital to getting the job done. A company at its most basic level is nothing more than a collection of individuals organizing themselves to accomplish a specific purpose. As each individual within the organization understands the benefits of alignment and then acts accordingly, the real power of alignment is tapped.

While Chapter 4 explored corporate-level strategies, this chapter will take a close look at personal strategies of alignment. Of course, it is the balance between both that allows the process to work best. It takes the positive efforts of both the corporation and individuals to achieve alignment.

The paradox here is that some people assume that past alignment ensures future alignment. The changing world of business means that even the highest performers and the best aligned employees need to make a conscious effort to stay aligned. Alignment involves constant action. This chapter is about action, about steps for improvement regardless of your present level of alignment with your company. If you're not taking action, then you've made a choice to leave your lifevision to the whims of chance. It's a bet I would advise against.

What's really in it for you?

Over the years, many people have asked me why they should align their personal lifevision with their company's purpose. "Won't that take away my individuality?" they ask. "If I'm going to devote so much energy to my company, what's in it for me?"

You spend a significant number of hours at work. It can be one of your most fulfilling lifevision communities. So why settle for anything less than full alignment and the benefits it can bring? The personal strategies of alignment can take you to a place of increased challenge, personal significance and productivity.

Psychologists tell us that we use only 20 to 30 percent of our potential energy and intellectual capacity. If this statistic is true, we all have great unused resources from which to draw. We all have room for improving our productivity and contribution to our company.

The Alignment Continuum

In my many years of experience as a consultant, I've found that most employees need some concrete formula for comparing themselves with their organizations. Although no equation can quantify such non-mathematical ideas as "purpose" or "mission," the Alignment Continuum has proven to be an effective tool for determining the compatibility of your purpose with that of your organization.

On one end of the continuum you'll find a total lack of alignment, while on the opposite end you'll find complete alignment. Determine where you and your organization are on the continuum by answering the following questions with scores between 1 (low) and 5 (high).

1) Do you believe that you are personally valued and respected as an employee of your organization? Is this value and respect demonstrated in tangible ways?

2) Do you believe in and wholeheartedly support the company's mission (why it exists, the customers it serves, and the needs it fulfills)?

3) Does the vision of the company (where it will be in the future) excite and inspire you? Can you see yourself playing a vital role in helping the company achieve that vision?

4) To what degree is your personal growth and development progressing at your company? Is the role you play at your company an active fulfillment of your personal purpose or an excellent stepping stone toward that fulfillment?

5) To what extent are the company's core values (the way it does business) in sync with your personal values (what you deeply believe)?

Total the scores from the five questions and plot your score on the continuum below.

The Alignment Continuum

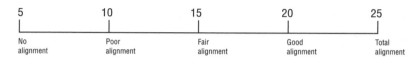

5	10	15	20	25
No alignment	Poor alignment	Fair alignment	Good alignment	Total alignment

Most of you will probably score somewhere in the middle range (13 to 20) on the continuum. This is commonly called the bell curve effect. In any given group, only a small percentage of the people will be in high alignment and a small percentage in low alignment. The majority of people end up somewhere in the middle. Regardless of where you fall on the continuum, your chances of increasing alignment are very good if you implement what I call personal alignment strategies.

Strategies Specifically for Those With Middle Scores (13-20) and Anyone Else Wishing to Increase Alignment

We can all improve our relationship with the organization we serve. Remember, you are the one who can make change happen. Here are six personal strategies to consider:

- Evaluate your attitude and approach toward work
- Evaluate your personal lifevision
- Develop a strategic alignment plan
- Assert yourself and your plan
- Promote your progress
- Celebrate your successes

Evaluate your attitude and approach toward work

Your first step toward improving alignment is to look in the mirror. In other words, you should first examine your own attitude and approach toward work. If you've felt unhappy with or unfulfilled in your work, it's easy to point a finger at someone or something else. "My company doesn't really care about me." "My supervisor is overbearing and difficult to please." "My coworkers aren't pulling their weight." These are examples of the way we blame our dissatisfaction on something other than ourselves. Have you really taken stock of your own contribution to the problem?

Although many factors can create an unpleasant work situation, it's important to ask yourself what you've done that might be part of the problem. The American culture has popularized victimization. When some aspect of our life goes wrong, we tend to look for someone or something to blame. We don't want to "own" our contribution to the problem. Just look at the number of frivolous lawsuits filed in the last decade. Whether you're a victim or not is really beside the point. Business, like life, is often unfair.

The most successful people in business – or any other field, for that matter – aren't afraid to accept responsibility for their actions. You must do the same. If you're failing to experience the personal growth you desire, or if you feel significantly out of sync with your organization or coworkers, ask yourself these questions:

- Is my attitude toward work productive?
- Is my current approach toward work really getting the job done?
- Have I really tried new ways of thinking and doing to make this job work?
- How much of my frustration is really my own fault?

Honest answers to these questions will help you approach alignment more clearly. You may be unaware that you yourself have created your unfulfilling work situation, either through your attitude or your approach.

Sue was the sales director for a $20 million manufacturer of fabricated components. She had a genuine desire to see the company succeed. Her knowledge of the industry made her an exceptional company resource, and her sales results were excellent. Over time, however, Sue managed to alienate a number of employees as well as some fellow division heads. Sue's approach to dealing with conflict was to insist on getting her way. What Sue didn't understand was just how difficult she was making things for everyone else.

Our consulting firm was asked to assist this company with a

planning process, and it was in the middle of this process that we discovered the problems they were having with Sue. As we began to work with Sue and the other division managers, we helped her to understand the negative impact of her work style. Although the realization was painful, Sue admitted that her excellent sales results were no excuse for the trouble she was causing throughout the organization. When confronted with the truth in a caring and respectful way, Sue realized that she was the problem. She needed to change her behavior in order to accomplish the company's goal of alignment and to achieve success over the long term.

Evaluate your personal lifevision

When people are out of alignment I always ask, "Have you taken the proper steps to discover and evaluate your personal lifevision?" Lack of alignment can result from an ill-defined personal lifevision or none at all. How can you be expected to align with your organization if you haven't made the effort to discover and define your personal lifevision? If you haven't taken the time or don't know how to define your lifevision, you can start right now. You can do it by working through Chapters 1, 2 and 3, and completing the Tool Kits at the end of each chapter.

Your work can be one of the best ways to express your personal purpose, your talents, and your strengths. As you evaluate your lifevision, you need to ask yourself if your work is fulfilling your personal purpose. The best way to answer that question is to evaluate the four purpose elements from Chapter 1 as they relate to your work:

 • *Your skills, talents and abilities:* These are the special competencies that you bring to the table, so your work should deliberately capitalize on them.

- *Your personality and temperament:* You have a one-of-a-kind personality. The way you process life and relate to others is distinctive, so your work should be a fit for your unique personality.

- *Your personal history and past experiences:* Your personal résumé is one of your most valuable work assets. By examining your past successes and learning experiences, you'll be able to focus your efforts in the present.

- *Your passions and interests:* Life is too short not to express your passions and interests through your work. You should be putting your effort into something that you can get excited or enthused about!

If after evaluating each of the above factors you find that your present employment doesn't integrate with your purpose, then you've reached a decision point. Is there another position in your organization for which you would be better suited? Is there a way that your skills can be put to a different use without changing employers? Do you need to look for another organization to which you can make a contribution?

Develop a creative strategic alignment plan

Assuming you would like to improve your alignment with your present employer, the next step is to develop a strategic alignment plan. Your plan should be authentically you, based on imaginative goals and strategies you've developed. The plan will basically consist of your personal lifevision, goals for each of your lifevision communities (your work in particular), and specific strategies you intend to implement to achieve your goals. In Chapter 6, I present an in-depth explanation of just how the planning process works, so I won't do that here. All alignment plans should take stock of the four elements mentioned in the above section.

Be creative and imaginative in generating ideas that will form the basis of your goals and strategies. Einstein said, "Imagination is more important than knowledge," and this is certainly true in creating your strategic alignment plan. In stimulating your imagination, try talking to people outside your normal sphere of friends and coworkers. Ask for advice. Try reading material you wouldn't normally consider. Sometimes great literature or poetry can stimulate the under-exercised parts of your imagination. Take a vacation away from your regular environment. If you work indoors, try the woods; if you live in the countryside, try the city. I've found that working puzzles and brain teasers forces me to think unconventionally.

Imagination is one of our most underrated tools. When you are creative, you can make almost any situation work in your favor. After you have generated some creative solutions, share them with a trustworthy colleague within your sphere of influence. Start creating an alignment plan to bridge the gap between your individual and corporate purposes.

Assert yourself and your plan

You can't wait for others to work on your behalf. You are in control of your own destiny, and no one cares as much about your success as you do. So decide to make your alignment work. The most difficult part of the battle is deciding to act. Once you assert your plan, stick to it.

Because you don't work in a vacuum, the success of your alignment plan will sometimes depend on the actions or reactions of your coworkers. Remember to remain flexible. Don't assume that everyone around you will be working on your schedule. If some parts of your plan don't go as well as expected, adjust them and move forward. Bear in mind that most alignment plans unfold somewhat differently, and over a longer period of time, than people anticipate.

Promote your progress

Some people say business has three cardinal rules for success: communicate, communicate, and communicate. While worklife isn't that simple, communication does play an crucial role in your ability to navigate toward alignment. As you progress, don't be afraid to share the news with others. Be discreet and modest, of course, but let people know what you are trying to achieve and what you are trying to change about yourself. Why? Because when you make sure others notice your new approach toward work, you also ensure that they will adjust their approach toward you.

This strategy has worked especially well for me throughout most of life, whether it was making sure my parents knew about and were supportive of my academic endeavors, or working closely with my college professors at Illinois State University, or ensuring that every one of my bosses understood that I wanted to learn, change, and grow in my work. The world isn't going to make an intentional effort to notice your achievements and changes. In fact, most of what we do happens in relative obscurity. You are your own best public relations person, so use it to your advantage.

Celebrate your successes

As you achieve each element of your plan, be sure to celebrate. In fact, you might want to make celebrations a deliberate part of your plan from the start. That way you won't forget to recognize your own progress and the changes in your circumstances and attitude.

Most of your celebrations can be simple: tickets to a ballgame or concert, dinner at a nice restaurant, a weekend trip. The point is to reward yourself for having achieved a significant change in your relationship with your organization. You're moving toward alignment, and that movement is improving your life.

Strategies Specifically for Those with High Scores (21-25)

If your alignment score is 21 or above, congratulations! While a top score doesn't mean you'll never face challenges to alignment, it does indicate that the prospects for ongoing alignment are strong. This level of alignment indicates that you're in a powerful position — one in which you can exert real leverage. Here are five personal strategies that will help you use this position wisely:

- Increase your self-awareness
- Refocus yourself on a daily basis
- Become a personal mentor
- Tap the power of innovation and creativity
- Take appropriate risks

Increase your self-awareness

Alignment today is no assurance of success tomorrow. The pace of change in the business world seems to be increasing exponentially. Just when you feel you've overcome one challenge, a new competitor, coworker, or customer changes the way you must do business. How do you deal with all the change, stay in alignment, and keep in top form? One important way is to become more self-aware.

As I noted in Chapter 2, the Center for Creative Leadership's comprehensive research shows that self awareness is one of the top characteristics of effective leadership. Effective people take the time to understand their strengths and weaknesses, both real and perceived. They desire to understand themselves and their behaviors completely. They seek out feedback regarding their actions and abilities from a whole spectrum of sources: people they supervise, bosses, personality profiles, skill and ability testing, personal friends, customers, etc. As your self-awareness increases, you'll have the information you need to make the personal changes and commitments necessary for ongoing success.

Refocus yourself on a daily basis

Getting the most from your work requires a daily commitment. To stay in alignment, you must refocus yourself mentally, physically, emotionally, and spiritually. Ask yourself the following questions:

- What is my personal lifevision?
- What am I doing to achieve that lifevision?
- What is getting in the way of that lifevision?

- Am I coming into better alignment with my company's purpose?

Set aside some uninterrupted time every day. You might want to refocus while jogging or riding a bicycle. Refocus over a cup of hot coffee or during a moment of quiet reflection in an empty room. Find a time, place, and activity that are right for you and then revisit them everyday. As you answer these broad questions, you will find considerably more focus in the details of your daily work.

Become a personal mentor

Aligning with your company is great, but becoming a champion for the cause is even better. The simplest way to influence the rest of your organization is to become a personal mentor. Mentoring is about sharing your story with others throughout the company. It's about taking an active role in assisting others in the synchronization of their work and their lifevision. Mentoring may sound like a lot of work, but you'll find it's easier to sustain as your coworkers begin to discover fulfillment in their work. Give away what you have, and good things will come back to you in ways you never expected.

To be an effective hands-on mentor:
- Assess your sphere of influence, whether at the company-wide, divisional, departmental, or team level.
- Work within your sphere to identify fellow employees who feel unfulfilled in their work or who seem to be out of alignment.

- Help those who express interest in the lifevision process to write their own lifevision statements and to align their personal and organizational purposes.

As your fellow employees experience alignment, they'll energize your workplace. Your team, your department, or your division will become more productive. Some of those who experience the process will become mentors for others, and you'll find that you've started a mini-revolution of attitudes and energy within your company.

Tap the power of innovation and creativity

"These days, everyone is smarter and faster. So, the key skill for remaining competitive, whether as a company or as a person in a company, is how you can innovate," says John Kao, an entrepreneur and lecturer on creativity. It is important for you to continually innovate in order to stay on the cutting edge of high performance and to remain in high alignment. Intentionally developing your creative muscles is the key. There are multiple ways to accomplish this.

A variety of creativity workshops are offered by training organizations today. These are excellent opportunities for exposure to totally new ways of thinking and working. Workshops help remove some of the mystery of being creative and help you get past the false notion that only certain types of people are really innovative. You'll be surprised at how many practical ways there are for applying creativity tools to your work.

There are also other ways to stimulate new ideas that don't cost much. Setting aside time on a daily or weekly basis to do some free thinking is one way. Some companies encourage employees to actually take work time and set it aside in this fashion. Read periodicals outside of your area of knowledge or field of work. You'll get a whole new perspective on how others view the world. Working puzzles works for some (including me!). Many puzzles and brain teasers are about seeing the presented problem from a different perspective. You have to change your way of thinking to solve the problem. As you stretch your mind in this way, you'll be able to do the same with the practical problems you're solving at work. Finally, I find that expanding my circle of relationships can reward me with a lot of fresh ideas. As you explore the art of conversation with others, sharing thoughts on meaningful topics with a variety of people inside and outside of work, you'll receive excellent insights that will change your way of thinking. You'll be equipped with new tools to confront the challenges of your work.

Take Appropriate Risks

High alignment is a great leverage point for achieving more within your organization, for who's in a better position to take a risk? Of course, your risks should always be calculated. Do your homework, and try to foresee all the possible consequences. I'm not encouraging you to be foolish. If you want to actively participate in your company's well-being, if you want to do more than simply follow orders, do your company and yourself a favor by pushing the envelope. Not only will your importance within your workplace grow, but your work will become more important within your life.

In 1994, just as I felt I was achieving true alignment with my work in Champaign, Illinois, my firm asked me to establish a consulting practice in San Diego. Talk about risk! I had lived in the Midwest my entire life, and my whole career had been geared toward building the Champaign consultancy. Now my firm wanted me to start from scratch in a new region of the country.

I took the risk, and now I can safely say that my choice has paid off. Because I brought all my previous experiments and experiences to this new consultancy, I was able to achieve an even greater alignment. I have felt even more satisfied with my work, and that satisfaction has translated into greater success in a variety of ways.

Strategies Specifically for Those With Low Scores (12 and under)

If you received a score of 12 or below on the alignment continuum, you are either seriously out of alignment or you've been hindered from getting the right information about your company's mission, vision, and values. Before you assume that your alignment is low and the situation has no hope, do take the time to ensure that you have the information you need. You may need to work at defining your organization's mission, vision, and values, so that you can honestly answer the questions on the alignment continuum.

If you have been able to gather the appropriate information and you've still scored rather low on the continuum, you've got some serious decisions to make. In all likelihood, you may need to start searching for another employer or consider alternatives to your present work situation. Leaving a company is always a difficult decision, so be as sure as you can that alignment is unlikely before taking such an irrevocable step. Nevertheless, if alignment seems impossible, you should consider making a change. Companies don't need employees who lack energy, motivation, and enthusiasm about the corporate direction. Likewise, you don't need work that's at odds with your lifevision.

As you contemplate leaving your current job and exploring other opportunities, here are some steps to take:

- Make sure you have completed the Tool Kit exercises at the end of each chapter and have done your best to define your personal lifevision.
- Take an inventory of all your skills and experience.
- Define the type of work opportunity that would best align with your lifevision.
- Assemble an action plan to identify and contact companies whose purposes match your own.
- Execute your plan.

Before making a change, consider these notes of caution:

Never leave too soon

Employees who have failed to fully assess their long-term potential or who want to avoid challenges often leave their jobs prematurely. I encourage anyone who is having difficulties to try to work through the problems first. Times of crisis often present unique opportunities for personal growth and achievement, even within the company.

Look into the future at your present company. Though promotions or new opportunities can be difficult to predict, they may also place you in a position to resolve your problems. Ask yourself if your present position represents a stepping stone to a more fulfilling position, even though the "stone" may be more steps away from that position than you would like.

Never burn bridges

Once you make the decision to leave, you may feel entitled to air your laundry list of grievances. While you may find the process cathartic, bite your tongue. These revelations will come back to haunt you. Never forget that business is about relationships and that you must continue to build relationships throughout your entire career. Positive connections to former employers and coworkers may prove invaluable down the road. You never know when you'll be doing business with these people again.

Avoid jumping out of the frying pan and into the fire

Never leave one unaligned situation only to enter another. Once you've made the decision to leave your present work, make sure you can align with your next potential employer. This may seem obvious, yet I've known many people who left organizations where they felt unfulfilled only to go to others where they felt equally unfulfilled. I recommend that you use the Alignment Continuum with all prospective employers. Answering the questions will require some additional homework, but you'll find the effort worthwhile.

Concluding Thoughts on Alignment

No matter what your situation in life and your score on the alignment continuum, alignment is hard work. After consulting with thousands of employees, I have found that even if people aren't experiencing fulfillment in their present jobs, most do have the potential for alignment. The causes of dissatisfaction often lie with the individual. When you take the time to explore your personal lifevision thoroughly and execute the strategies outlined in this chapter, achieving alignment can become a reality.

The grass is not always greener on the other side of the fence. If you have the right tools and are willing to take the time to reflect on your life's purpose, you will often discover that your destiny can be fulfilled right where you are. Suppose that, like many employees, your organization isn't in perfect alignment with your personal purpose. Given the high economic, emotional, and mental costs of finding a new job or career, you need to ask yourself if alignment is indeed possible in the long run.

My experience has taught me that many of us gravitate toward the type of work that is right for us. We may not always end up where we had intended to go, but we must trust our instincts. Even after I had worked in the business world for several years, I truly believed I would someday leave corporate America and become a missionary. I was under the mistaken impression that unless I joined the ministry full-time I would never be able to help others improve their lives in a meaningful way. I failed to see that I had gravitated toward business because I was good at it. I didn't have to throw away my hard-earned (and expensive) education and training. After I finally sorted through my confusion, I knew that my current work could be meaningful and that I could make a difference in people's lives. I redefined my lifevision in terms of a new approach to my occupation and have been challenged and fulfilled ever since. Does that mean I'll always be expressing my lifevision through my current occupation and employer? Maybe not. My lifevision may change and evolve over time, but at each step of the way I want to be in alignment with whatever organization I serve.

Chapter 5 Tool Kit

Exercise 5-1: *Creativity Exercise*

Write one or two creative paragraphs explaining who you are **without** referring to any of the following:

> Education
>
> Job/Career
>
> Hobbies
>
> Pastimes
>
> Sports Interests
>
> Spouse
>
> Children
>
> Geography
>
> Specific talents
>
> Titles

Exercise 5-2: *Creating Your Innovative Alignment Plan*

Now that you've had an opportunity to be creative, it's time to put your innovative thinking ability to work. In answering the questions below, get creative and stretch your thinking a bit!

1. Take another look at your score on the alignment continuum. Why did you receive that particular score? In other words, what have you or your organization done to produce your present state of alignment?

2. Are you satisfied with your alignment score, or could it be better? How much better?

3. What are others in your organization doing to achieve alignment? Do you notice certain behavior patterns in high-performing coworkers?

4. Describe some past actions you've taken to increase your alignment with your company. Are you still taking these same steps today?

5. As you think of your specific talents, competencies, personality, and temperament, what are some innovative ways you can think of to increase your

alignment? What ideas could you get excited about and put some energy into?

6. What can others in your organization do to help you increase your alignment?

Chapter 6

Power Tools for Alignment
Strategies for Balance and Integration Outside of Work That Will Increase Your Alignment at Work

"A house divided against itself cannot stand."
—Jesus

"Man cannot do right in one department whilst he is occupied in doing wrong in any other department. Life is one indivisible whole."
—Gandhi

Let me tell you about a special person I know. Dianne is one of those individuals who keeps raising the height of the bar for the rest of us to jump over. She serves as one of three members of an executive leadership team for a large, growing, nonprofit organization. One of her key roles on the team is providing visionary and inspirational thought leadership. She is constantly reading a spectrum of books to glean "best practices" and novel, insightful approaches. She is also a powerful communicator of the organization's ideas. I've witnessed her ability to hold an audience in rapt attention as she expounds on vision and hope for the future.

Her job alone would be enough to exhaust most of us, yet she is one of the most devoted mothers I know. Her five children, ranging from elementary to college age, receive her constant attention and encouragement. With both academic and athletic talents in the family's genes, she finds the time to attend one event after another. She also serves on the Parent Teacher Association and is involved in the lives of her neighbors. Their house is known as Activity Central for the neighborhood children. Finally, she is an encouraging example of spiritual strength for those in her sphere of influence. Through a thirty-year-long commitment to personal renewal, she has climbed the mountain of spiritual leadership, providing an inspiring example to many.

What's her secret? One of her main strengths is the ability to balance and integrate her lifevision communities so that each supports her central purpose of "bringing wholeness to individual lives, one by one." In particular, her work role has reached new heights through her commitment to each of her other roles. Instead of each interpersonal role competing for her time, they work in synergy with each other and are centered around a common theme — her lifevision. In the process, she is free to fulfill her unique destiny in each of her roles!

You, too, can bring a new dimension to your work and increase your opportunity for alignment by balancing and integrating each of your lifevision communities. Said another way, what you do outside of work — bringing your lifevision communities into balance and integrating them — may be the best thing you do for you work. Balance and integration eliminate wasted time and energy, bringing our lifevision communities into harmony with each other. They are what I call the "power tools" for achieving alignment. As your lifevision roles come into better agreement and relationship with each other, the quality of your work has to go up. It's similar to what the professional medical community has discovered in the last ten to twenty years. Eastern civilizations have practiced "holistic medicine" for centuries, and the western medical community now appears to be acknowledging its validity. "Holistic" means treating the whole person, not just physical symptoms. Emotional pain does indeed affect your physical body. Likewise, when there's pain or dysfunction in one of your lifevision communities, your work is affected. Integration and balance are two of the tools that can keep you healthy in each of your lifevision communities, and the result is higher productivity and success at work!

Lifevision Diagrams 6a and 6b:

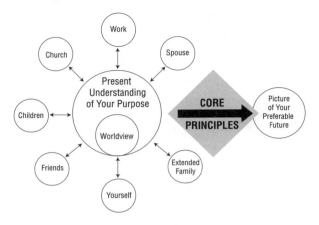

6a — Compartmentalized Lifevision Communities

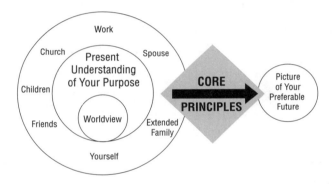

6b — Balanced and Integrated Lifevision Communities

Principle: *To be most effective in your work, balance and integrate all of your lifevision communities.*

Paradox: *The long term payoff may not be obvious in the short term.*

The two diagrams show different ways of thinking about our

lifevision communities. The first illustration shows our lifevision communities as separate compartments, neatly segregated from one another. The second picture illustrates a more healthy approach — one of balance and integration that draws your lifevision communities closer to the central purpose of your life. Instead of remaining separate compartments, your lifevision communities connect to each other and your purpose. If each of your interpersonal roles can work in harmony with each other via balance and integration, then your effectiveness in each arena will be enhanced. However, increasing your integration and balance without a meaningful framework becomes merely an exercise in efficiency. Your lifevision is the framework.

You need to understand that each of your lifevision communities has an impact on the others and contributes to or detracts from the accomplishment of your life purpose. Your life is an interactive system. As such, advances in one lifevision community, while properly integrated and balanced with the others, can yield tremendous results. You may initially resist the idea of balance and integration, and that is because the long-term payoff may not be obvious in the short term. For example, certain aspects of balancing and integrating may seem to run counter to making us more productive in our work. It may seem like nonsense to schedule an afternoon off to visit the zoo with your children when you have so many pressing things to worry about at work. Yet the renewal and strength gained by doing something like this can more than compensate for the work time "lost."

I encourage you to open your mind to these ideas. Spending quality time in each of your lifevision communities, if each is supporting your overall lifevision, can bring a new richness and depth to your work experience. You'll approach problem solving from a fresh perspective. You'll appreciate challenges from a different angle. You'll be renewed with energy and vitality. In this chapter, we'll look at what integration and balance are, why they are important, and practical strategies for achieving them.

Defining Integration

All of us want to be people of integrity. Integrity conveys honesty, forthrightness, nobility, and strength. But did you know that it shares the same root word as integration? They really mean the same thing: oneness, unity, and commonality. To be a person of integrity is to live an integrated life and to be congruent in all of our lifevision communities. They all point in the same direction. In light of this, I like to define integration as:

> *Understanding that your life consists of multiple lifevision communities, but rather than treating these roles as separate compartments, bringing them into congruity with each other around a central life theme — your lifevision.*

You, like many others, may have become very comfortable with "compartmentalizing" your life. That is, you think of your life as having separate compartments of work, family, personal time, and so on. It sure makes life easier to deal with, doesn't it? You can simply "seal off" a compartment you're struggling with and focus on an area where you're doing better. If you're having trouble in your marriage, you can concentrate on and feel good about your work. Or if your relationship with your children isn't too hot, you can ease the pain by your involvement in the United

Way. Compartments seem to be great for organizing and simplifying life.

Yet I believe, and the lives of many successful people have shown, that integration is a better, faster way to your preferable future. If we can make each lifevision community support the others, and if we can be congruent from one role to the other, we will go a long way toward achieving personal success. The lines between our life roles will blur and the compartment walls will come down. If you have bought into the compartmentalization paradigm, perhaps it's time for a paradigm shift!

Integration is about building a life around a central lifevision and then establishing goals in each of our lifevision communities that support that overall life purpose.

What does integration not mean? It doesn't mean:

- setting the same goals and pursuing the same strategies in each lifevision community
- combining each of your lifevision communities in an amorphous melting pot
- losing the distinctiveness and unique expression of each lifevision community

Although your roles should all center around a common life theme, you should establish unique goals for each interpersonal role. This will actually enhance the fulfilling of your lifevision, and will allow you to attack it from multiple angles and in various ways. You don't need to blend each role together so that they are all the same. In fact, keeping the individuality of each of your lifevision communities is what brings a depth and richness to your everyday life experience. Integration doesn't mean losing that diversity; rather, it means using that diversity to support a common end result.

Defining Balance

Living an integrated life requires a healthy dose of balance. I must confess that this is one area that is a constant struggle for me. That's because balance doesn't mean equal time for each lifevision community. It is much more dynamic that that. I like to define balance this way:

Devoting the appropriate amount of time and energy to each respective lifevision community, in dynamic proportion to the others.

Balance requires you to ask yourself: "At this particular point in my life, how much time and energy is appropriate for each lifevision community?" The answer to that question always changes with the seasons of life and may change as frequently as week to week! Balance requires constant awareness of your lifevision communities and their relationships with each other. Your alternative to balancing is to allow one role to encroach upon the others, or to haphazardly let your time be absorbed by whatever roles demand it at the moment. Neither of these alternatives will work if the picture of your preferable future includes success in each lifevision community.

Balance is illustrated repeatedly in nature. Predator and prey. Planting and harvesting. Life and death. Summer and winter. Motion and rest. The many delicate systems of nature must operate in balance in order to function properly. In spite of the constant reminders in nature, most of us seem to have difficulty staying balanced. Balance requires an effort on your part: you must take control of life as opposed to allowing it to take control of you. It means embracing more "both/and" and not as much "either/or." For example, you want to say things like, "Both my career and my family are important to me, so I will spend time with each," as opposed to, "I must choose either my job or my family, so I will choose to emphasize my family."

Balance doesn't necessarily mean an equal amount of time and energy for each role or activity. It does mean that if we consider a lifevision community important in our life, we need to spend an appropriate amount of time in it. That is not always easy. It may require changing deeply ingrained behavior patterns, patterns that are not getting us where we want to go.

Why Integration and Balance?

Understanding the definitions of integration and balance can enable you to see some of the powerful benefits that come from shifting your paradigm away from compartmentalization:

- enhancing your work experience and increasing your opportunity for alignment
- increasing your effectiveness in each of the other lifevision communities
- helping you "walk the talk" of becoming a person of principle

Enhancing your work experience and increasing your opportunity for alignment

Perhaps one of the most significant upsides of balancing and integrating your lifevision communities will be the increased effectiveness of your work. I've discovered that the quality of thought and energy in my work has risen dramatically as I've become more committed to balancing my lifevision communities around my central purpose. Time spent in my non-work roles has been rewarded by the increased effectiveness of my work. Some of my best work ideas come from spending quiet personal time and from interacting with personal friends in small group settings. I now regularly expect my other lifevision communities to freshen my perspective and give me the fuel I need to do well at work.

Paul is an example of someone who has become much more effective in his work because of his commitment to balancing and integrating all of his life roles. He is the director of a teen outreach program. He has a passion for working with kids and enjoys helping them through their often turbulent adolescent years. He spends extra evening and weekend hours helping them solve their personal problems. As dedicated he is to his career, he is also a model of balance and integration. He takes time with his wife and three children to enjoy activities like boating, water skiing, hunting, and playing board games. When work gets especially demanding, he deliberately schedules time with his family. Paul also finds time to serve as an elder in his church, work with community groups, exercise, keep a journal, and maintain a personal daily quiet time.

I'm convinced that Paul's balance and integration are what make him the great program director that he is. Because of his balanced commitment to family, church, community, and himself, he has abundant energy to lend to his work. As he devotes time to the other areas of his life, his passion for his job is renewed. While most people who work with youth drop out after one to two years of service (and the dropout rate is close to 100 percent after five years), Paul is still going strong after twenty years! He's one of only a handful of people in his field with such a long tenure.

Increasing your effectiveness in each of the other lifevision communities

As you center your interpersonal roles around your lifevision, the quality of what you accomplish in each role is bound to increase. I've seen this phenomenon first hand in the lives of many people, including my own. One of the best examples is my friend David. He is the chief executive officer of a manufacturing company in Illinois. David is one of the finest business people I know. He is a shrewd dealmaker, yet is compassionate and caring of his employees. He has made the commitment to build each of his skill areas over the years to the point that he has a broad knowledge of marketing, finance, operations, human resources, and strategy. But I am most inspired by the balance and integration that David lives out every day, bringing his effectiveness in each role to new levels.

Over the last six years I've watched David live a commitment to balancing and integrating his work, community, family, and personal roles. He regularly takes a lunch hour with his wife. Although his relationship with her has many other dimensions, I view this simple act as symbolic of their overall relationship. I admire any CEO who can take time of out of a busy work day to enjoy conversation and fellowship with his life partner.

David also alters his work schedule to ensure that he spends plenty of time with his four daughters. If you talk to his girls, you'll know that they are head over heels in love with their father. On top of that, David has been very involved in leading small groups and serving on the financial advisory board of his church. His pastor told me that David is a rare and refreshing individual — committed, caring, and facing life with a great attitude. As involved as David is in each of these interpersonal roles, he also has an amazing commitment to himself. He exercises and eats right, has a daily quiet time, and regularly sets goals that fit into his life purpose. David's increasing balance and integration have brought him newfound effectiveness and a depth of quality in each of his life roles. In so doing, he's become a great inspiration to me as I seek to do the same.

Helping you "walk the talk" of becoming a person of principle

How do you consistently walk the talk? What is the secret to living by principles (see Chapter 3), so that what you want to do is actually what you end up doing? I like to think of balance and integration as providing part of the answer to these questions. If you can achieve congruency between your personal, community, family, and career roles, you will go a long way toward walking the talk. As your roles balance and integrate with one another, the incongruities from role to role are removed. For me, my relationship with my wife, Toni, is one of the most powerful mechanisms for exposing my inconsistencies from role to role, helping me make changes and encouraging me along the way. I often share an accomplishment or challenge from one of my other lifevision communities with my wife. She offers perspective on the issue that is totally different than my own. Most importantly, she consistently helps me dismantle the false ego I allow my accomplishments to create. Just when I think I've arrived, she gently shows me that I still have plenty of work to do in becoming a person of principle.

Paradox: How Do Balance and Integration Fit with Diverse Interests?

As with the other principles outlined in this book, the principle of balancing and integrating your life comes with an interesting paradox. There is a certain pleasure and self satisfaction in pursuing diverse interests. Put another way, "variety is the spice of life."

Having diverse interests provides a special intellectual and emotional stimulation. The more things we expose ourselves to, the richer our lives become for the experience. For instance, you might simultaneously pursue the hobby of stamp collecting, enjoy surfing the Internet, and serve on your neighborhood homeowner's association. Each of these activities can bring a certain satisfaction, while filling your time with variety and change of pace. The mistake is made, however, in the failure to step back from the pursuits in which we're involved to ask, "Are each of these making a valuable contribution to my lifevision?" Put another way, is there a better way to spend your time, so that you have a better chance of accomplishing your life goals? As you ask these questions, you might find that certain activities aren't really giving you any payback. In other words, they're not moving you any closer to achieving your lifevision.

If you can view the whole group of your life roles and activities from the bigger picture perspective, you begin to see that they can indeed integrate and balance with one another to support your overall lifevision. Once you step back to see your roles and activities in this light, certain things can happen. You might find a role that really doesn't belong, that is causing more trouble than it's worth, or that no longer fits with your current understanding of your lifevision. If a particular role is getting in the way of integration — in other words, it just doesn't fit well with the others — then it's probably time to make a change. Likewise, if a certain role is getting in the way of balance by consuming too much time, then a change needs to be made.

Trouble Spots With Balance and Integration

In terms of **integration**, the roles of community involvement and personal leisure pursuits seem to be trouble spots for people. It's easy to say "yes" to a community or social role that really doesn't fit with your lifevision. It's important to be involved in these types of roles, but we need to be selective about which ones we commit to. For leisure pursuits, I have observed many people making poor choices with their time allocation. Since moving to California, where the weather and outdoor amenities are quite accommodating, I've noticed that people seem to be filling their time with a variety of leisure pursuits. While everyone needs recreation, I have to wonder whether some folks are making any progress at all on fulfilling their lifevision. They seem too busy filling up their time with leisure pursuits.

As far as **balance** goes, most people seem to be getting into trouble with their work or career roles. Statistics indicate that the average person is spending more time at work these days than they did a decade or two ago. As companies push for performance increases and try to do more with less, they seem to be making increased demands on employees. It's not hard to understand why so many of us believe that our work is encroaching on our other life roles. The lifevision communities that suffer the most from this abuse are the spouse and family roles. It's why many a marriage hits the rocks at the same time a career peaks. Family and work roles can simultaneously become very demanding. It is a difficult tension to manage. If you aren't committed to balance, or if you're not seeing each of your roles in the context of supporting a larger lifevision, then you might find yourself completely abandoning one role in favor of another. Oftentimes this means we choose work and walk away from our family roles. Consequently, we create a tragic trail of broken relationships in the wake of our narrow-minded choices.

Rather than seeing your roles as competing for slices of your time, envision them as mutually supporting a common lifevision. This requires a commitment to balance and integration. While that commitment can be difficult, the results can be astounding. I believe that properly managing the natural tension between roles through integration and balance can result in increased effectiveness and richness in each role. Not only will our roles cease to compete, they'll enrich and strengthen each other.

How to Make Balance and Integration Work

Making balance and integration work for you calls for a practical implementation framework. Such a framework can help you break down your "big picture" lifevision into more bite-sized tasks. It is these smaller sized, daily actions that ultimately become the building blocks of something more significant and meaningful.

Implementing effective strategies for accomplishing practical actions can be very difficult. You may prefer to "go with the flow" when organizing a daily schedule or, managing a "to do" list, moving items from one day to the next and crossing off completed tasks with a sense of pride and satisfaction might be more your style. Neither of these two approaches is really effective in the long run. "Going with the flow" won't ensure the accomplishment of your most important goals or fulfill your lifevision. And "to do" lists tend to focus on the short term and on small details. Even the best "to do" list can't ensure consistent progress toward your larger life goals. You need a procedure for integrating and coordinating the activities of each of your lifevision communities. While time/life management experts have addressed some aspects of effective balance and integration, I would like to emphasize the following keys for really making it work:

- *Annually*—Putting your lifevision into writing
- *Annually*—Reexamining your lifevision communities
- *Annually*—Establishing major themes for each lifevision community
- *Annually*—Establishing major goals for each lifevision community
- *Weekly*—Establishing strategies for achieving your goals
- *Daily*—Acting in accordance with your weekly strategies

Annually—Putting your lifevision into writing

I hope that you'll decide to draft your first lifevision statement in the process of interacting with this book. The Tool Kits at the end of each chapter and the Appendix provide all the tools needed to put together your first lifevision statement. This is really the first step toward fulfilling your lifevision, and it is the first strategy of making balance and integration happen. Before we can balance and integrate around a central theme, we need to articulate exactly what that theme is. There is something very powerful about putting your thoughts, hopes, and dreams into writing. You're setting yourself up to be accountable! Putting your lifevision into writing — documenting your purpose, your lifevision communities, and your intentions to close the principle gap in your life — is a fundamental first step.

Just as important as drafting your initial lifevision statement is the annual review and updating of it. The experiences of the previous year will give you a new perspective on the future. Undoubtedly, things will have unfolded in a different manner than you expected. You may have encountered one or more life-changing events that significantly shifted the vision of where you intend to go. Hopefully, you will have made good progress on meeting several of your lifevision goals.

You may want to revise your lifevision more frequently, but annual updates work best for most people. The final weeks of the calendar year have always worked best for me. Many companies give their employees extra time off, or you may elect to take a little vacation time around the holidays. Instead of just making a New Year's resolution or two, why not do something far more meaningful?

Annually—Reexamining your lifevision communities

When you review your lifevision statement, you should also reexamine your lifevision communities. Ask yourself if these roles are coordinating with and contributing toward your lifevision. Do you need to eliminate any roles, or add new ones? If you have trouble saying no, you should pay special attention to any extraneous roles you may have taken on during the previous year. Overextension is an easy way to fall out of alignment.

I've struggled with the problem of saying no for most of my life. I suppose this is mostly due to my distaste for confrontation and rejection. I say "yes" to please and placate others. In addition, it probably has something to do with the fact that I enjoy doing so many things. Whether it's speaking, writing, working with people, doing a bit of theater, being with my family, taking interesting vacations, or reading books, it's hard for me to say no. But I have to, and so do you. Let me illustrate further.

On a missions trip to the Czech Republic in 1992, the missions team leader, John, asked me to list all my current roles and to think about a theme for my life (this event was actually the starting point of what has become this book!). Then he asked me to examine whether or not those roles were supporting or contributing to my theme. He told me to calculate the number of hours per week I was spending on each role and to decide whether that amount of time was appropriate in light of my life's theme. It was surprising to see on paper how many things I had gotten myself involved in!

At a breakfast meeting with my brother Ben a few months later, I started filling in details of my first lifevision statement that I had started in Prague. Together we bounced around the idea of a business consulting process that would help middle-market companies achieve high performance and long-term success. With John's and Ben's help, I conceived of a plan to develop a set of tools for companies and employees faced with managing large amounts of change. This was the formal beginning of my life-work — my lifevision.

It was during the development of this first lifevision that I realized I was overextending myself. I was committed to ten different lifevision communities. I felt so pressured and burned out that I was ineffective in nearly every role. Although I hate to say no, I decided to resign as the Board Chairman of a local community organization, declined to run again for Homeowner's Association President, and gave up an extra role at work. In the past several years, I've been careful to limit my lifevision communities to no more than six or seven. Streamlining my life in this way has restored my energy and helped me to focus much better.

Annually—Establishing major themes for each lifevision community

I highly recommend establishing a major theme for each of your lifevision communities. A theme succinctly states your vision and emphasis for a role during the upcoming year. For example, here are the themes I used for each of my roles in 1997:

Theme for the role of consulting partner: Leadership. I want to be a leader that mentors and develops his team, not just leads them from a distance.

Theme for the role of father: Encouragement. I want to

emphasize encouragement and downplay criticism for each of my three daughters. In so doing, I'll help them set appropriate life goals, and I'll participate in shaping their destinies.

Theme for the role of husband: Friendship. I want to reestablish myself as my wife's best friend. Despite the fast pace of our lives, we need to take time to participate in each other's lives.

Theme for the role of church leader: Challenge. I want to inspire and challenge members of my discussion group to discover and align their lifevisions. I also want to encourage them to avoid complacency by taking risks in their personal, social, and business roles.

Theme for the role of friend and neighbor: Accountability. I want to develop one or two close relationships that are open, honest, and replenishing. In particular, I want the relationship(s) to be one of accountability, where we mutually agree to help each other achieve our lifevisions.

Theme for the role of Me: Renewal. This year, I want to renew myself in the some very specific ways: running three times a week, fasting once a week, engaging in a more focused, spiritual quiet time on a daily basis, and keeping my emotions healthy.

Themes establish a framework that will help you in the next

step, establishing goals. Without a theme for each role, your goals may lack focus. Establishing themes requires little time, but it's invaluable. If you set a theme for each role that directly relates to your goals, I guarantee that at the end of the year you'll be closer to fulfilling your lifevision.

Annually—Establishing major goals for each lifevision community

After you have reviewed and updated your roles and developed a theme for each one, you should establish goals for the year. What do you want to accomplish? What will best help you accomplish your lifevision? For each lifevision community, I recommend three to six goals that are S-M-A-R-T:

S – Specific. Goals should be as specific as possible.

M – Measurable. Goals should be measurable so you are able to evaluate them, whether or not they have been achieved.

A – Action-oriented. Goals should require you to act.

R – Realistic. Goals should be challenging yet achievable. Setting your sights too high will only lead to frustration and disappointment, but setting them too low will lead to stagnation.

T – Tied to your lifevision. All of your goals should ultimately relate to your overall lifevision.

Here are examples of some of my own goals for various roles:

Consulting Partner

1. Hold regular meetings with entire consulting team.
2. Help key managers develop a strategic plan for their functional area.
3. Keep an updated list of client needs.

Father

1. Schedule two or three memorable events during the year for the entire family.
2. Schedule a family fun time once every one to two weeks.
3. Actively support and participate in each daughters' schooling and extracurricular activities.

Husband

1. Schedule a date once every two to three weeks.
2. Have a deeper-level, meaningful conversation at least once a week.
3. Attempt to be more spontaneous with small gestures of kindness.

Me

1. Read two books per month on assorted topics.
2. Exercise three times a week.
3. Become more focused in my daily quiet time, using a mixture of meditative reading, prayer, and quiet reflection.

Weekly—Establishing strategies for achieving your goals

I can't overstate the importance of establishing strategies on a weekly basis to help you achieve each of your goals. This is the critical bridge between your "big picture" lifevision and goals and really making it all happen. In order to establish your weekly strategies, set aside a small amount of time on Sunday afternoon or Monday morning for planning the upcoming week. You'll find that the process usually takes only ten to twenty minutes. While most planning can be done on a weekly basis, you may want to start each month by scheduling some of your relationship-centered and replenishing activities that require prior arrangements.

Here are some guidelines to follow during your weekly planning session:

1) Review your lifevision statement and the goals you have set for each lifevision community. This review is a critical part of translating your lifevision into daily action. Ask yourself:
   - Were my activities last week supportive of my lifevision? If not, how can I move in that direction?
   - Am I balancing and integrating each of my lifevision communities? If not, what adjustments should I make?
   - Are each of my roles currently contributing to my lifevision? If not, what adjustments should I make?
   - Are each of my annual goals still pertinent? If not, what adjustments should I make?

• What have I learned recently that might expand, clarify, or change my lifevision?

2) Establish weekly strategies for achieving certain goals. The specific strategies you select and the particular goals you work on will vary from week to week.

3) Review all meetings and events already scheduled from prior weeks. Are you able to keep each of these commitments as well as accomplish each of your strategies?

4) Keeping steps 2 and 3 in mind, schedule activities that support your objectives by reserving blocks of space on your calendar. I recommend using some type of weekly planner. In your planner, you actually commit blocks of time for accomplishing your weekly goals, just the same as you set aside time for appointments. This ensures that what is most important to you — the goals that are going to help you achieve your lifevision — become a part of your schedule.

Daily—Acting in accordance with your weekly strategies

The rubber meets the road in your daily actions. You must consciously act in accordance with your weekly plan. I recommend that you begin the day by reviewing three things: your calendar, your "to do" list, and the strategies you established at the beginning of the week. What are the most important things you should accomplish for today? If you aren't accomplishing your weekly objectives, ask yourself why and determine whether you can get back on track. Most of us allow the tyranny of the urgent or the onslaught of minutiae to get in the way of accomplishing our weekly strategies.

Your calendar, "to do" list, and weekly objectives will overlap, and some items will conflict. Remain focused on your weekly objectives, but remember to stay flexible. Everyone has a different style of working and keeping commitments for the day. Don't feel you have to conform to any artificial rules.

Concluding thoughts on balance and integration

The process of translating the concepts of balance and integration into practical daily action takes time, energy, and commitment. You must be persistent, patient, and flexible. As you make progress in balancing and integrating, you will begin to experience increased effectiveness in each of your lifevision communities. As you execute each of the above strategies, particularly in your work role, the quality of your work will increase. This strategic framework will facilitate alignment with your company and its purpose. As you become more focused on your life purpose, translating big picture goals into daily actions, you can't help but increase your alignment with your company.

Chapter 6 Tool Kit

Exercise 6-1: *Lifevision Community Analysis*

For each of your current lifevision communities, provide the following information:

Lifevision Community	Hours Spent Per Week	Do You Enjoy?	Does it Support Your Lifevision?	Does it Fit with Other Roles?

In reviewing the chart, ask the following questions:

1. Are you devoting the right amount of time to roles that will really get you where you want to go?

2. Are you involved in roles that are not contributing to your lifevision?

3. Are you enjoying your roles? Why or why not?

4. Do one or more roles receive an inordinate amount of your time?

Exercise 6-2: *Balance and integration*

Now that you have completed Exercise 6-1, it's time to ask some more questions about balance and integration. How can you make these "academic concepts" more practical and relate them to your life?

1. How have you treated your lifevision communities (your interpersonal roles) as separate compartments? Explain.

2. What are some of the benefits of compartmentalizing? What are some of the downsides?

3. Has your integration of roles increased over time? Why or why not?

4. When you think of better integrating your lifevision, what obstacles do you think will get in the way?

5. How can you better integrate your lifevision communities?

6. What does balance mean to you?

7. What have been the most difficult things about balancing multiple roles?

8. How can you better balance your lifevision communities?

Part III

Renewing Your Lifevision

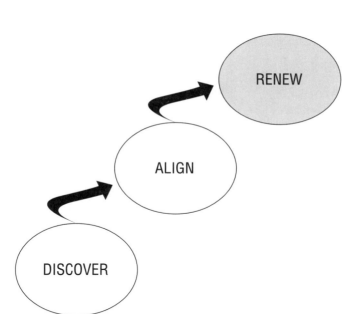

Chapter 7

Managing Obstacles and Change

"The ultimate measure of a man is not where he stands in moments of comfort and convenience, but where he stands at times of challenge and controversy."

—Martin Luther King, Jr.

No one particularly enjoys a financial difficulty, a communication breakdown with a close friend, or a career setback. Yet how you choose to deal with these types of situations can be significant in determining your ultimate success in life. From a broader perspective, life can be viewed as one big obstacle course, full of challenging experiences. Navigating the obstacle course with a clear sense of purpose and direction, accompanied by an attitude of persistence, is usually the key to experiencing a positive outcome. If you have a cloudy sense of your purpose, or you complain every time a new barrier stands in your way, the end result is likely to fall far short of where you wanted to be.

Thomas Edison tried hundreds of ideas for inventing the light bulb before hitting on the one that worked. Abraham Lincoln experienced several lost elections, the death of his mother, and business failure prior to becoming the most celebrated president in the history of the United States. Fred Smith, founder of Federal Express, hopped a plane to Vegas, winning enough to meet an upcoming payroll when he had exhausted all other options early in the company's history. In his successful quest to plant the missions of California, Father Junipero Serra battled a serious leg infection and strong resistance from Spanish army officers, as well as food shortages and drought. Science, religion, politics, and history are full of examples of people who faced great challenge in pursuit of a specific mission. Their clear sense of purpose, joined by an attitude of perseverance, yielded triumph in the end.

Lifevision Diagram 7: *"Managing obstacles and change"*

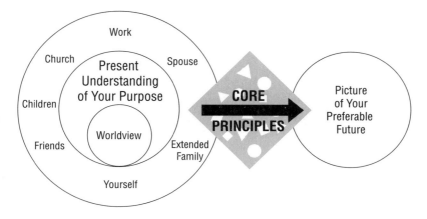

Principle: *See obstacles as growth opportunities. Use them to become more committed to and more focused on your lifevision.*

Paradox: *In the middle of dealing with obstacles, you don't always notice the growth opportunity.*

This diagram illustrates the reality that we all confront on our journey: plenty of obstacles, change, and challenges. Hoping they won't happen is simply a waste of time. You are much better off embracing the obstacles as opportunities for learning.

Life is going to throw you curve balls. You're going to have barricades placed right in the middle of the road you thought you were supposed to take. As you move toward the picture of your preferable future, you'll be faced with obstacles that will threaten to knock you on your back. If you don't concentrate on continuing your forward progress toward a specific vision of the future, you'll probably end up somewhere else!

Without a well-defined purpose or a clear conception of where you're headed, obstacles will divert you to a new path and a different end result. You'll end up taking a different direction, perhaps one entirely unintended. I'm not saying that life's serendipitous opportunities are all bad. Indeed, along the way you'll no doubt experience healthy diversions. That's fine, as long as you can get back on track or adapt in the right way. It's important to recognize when a problem or challenge is causing you to lose direction and focus. Then, as you see the challenge for what it is, and use it as a learning opportunity, you can strengthen your forward progress toward your lifevision.

Our character is formed in the crucible of challenge and change

Earlier, I talked about the difficulty I've had committing to regular physical exercise. Why has it been such a struggle? Simply put, exercise is hard work. It involves pushing our body beyond the comfort zone. That means there's a price to pay for getting in shape. And for some that price is too high, so they just don't do it.

When we push our body, it pushes back on us. That is the principle of physical resistance, the successful result of which is better muscle tone, less flab, and better overall health. But resistance means pain and struggle. We have to endure the pain to get the gain. A healthy body means hard work!

Life's problems and challenges are like the resistance we encounter in our bodies during physical exercise. In fact, you might think of relationship problems, communication blunders, and financial hardships as the "weights in the gym of life." If we view our problems in this way, we will be encouraged to work through them and see the challenges for what they are: a resistance which can help us sharpen our focus and build character. The payoff can be tremendous.

My friend David (from Chapter 6) is a good example of this principle. Formerly a world class pole vaulter, David became well acquainted with the principle of physical resistance through endless workout and training sessions. But the challenge of training for the Olympics has paled in comparison to the real-life battles of running a large manufacturing business.

For many years, the company struggled with falling profit margins, increasing competitive pressure, inventory management difficulties, and a host of other problems. Through it all, David maintained a positive attitude, using each setback as a lesson to make changes, both in the company and in himself. He strengthened his commitment to his faith, his family, and his friends during these turbulent times. He had plenty of opportunities to give up or to cast blame. But he chose to work through the challenges, convinced of a clear vision for what the company could one day achieve.

In the last couple of years the company has experienced a great turnaround, and the business is thriving today. Revenue is growing, profits are up, inventory is well managed, and the future looks bright. Much of this is to David's credit, though he is quick to share that credit with many others. To hear David tell it, those lean years made him much wiser and more mature as a businessman, as well as a more grateful and humble human being.

If there is a lesson to be learned, it is that David embraced the resistances he encountered and worked through them. Through years of multiple resistances, with no apparent light at the end of the tunnel, he kept moving forward with a persistent and positive attitude. Today David enjoys some of the fruit of his long years of labor, but he doesn't project the attitude of having arrived. He knows better than that. He knows that the future will continue to bring tough business problems and personal challenges, but his character has been molded and made strong. He is ready to thrive no matter what the future holds.

Being a lifelong learner

One of the keys to seeing obstacles as opportunities instead of threats involves adopting an attitude of lifelong learning. This means always being open to new frontiers, accepting and integrating new ideas into your worldview, and reshaping your life-vision as it unfolds over time. The future will always happen differently than you think. Things won't transpire exactly like you had thought. The timeframe may be much longer than you had hoped, or major unplanned events may impose themselves on your life. Yet if you remain a lifelong learner, always open to blending your planned purpose with life's serendipitous events, you'll find new perspectives and opportunities in every season of life.

Being a lifelong learner helps us to overcome a powerful, yet largely unexamined, phenomenon that shapes many of our lives. This is the phenomenon of inertia. When an attitude of lifelong learning and growing is absent, humans have a tendency to stay with what they are most familiar for an indefinite period of time — even to the point when the path becomes a well worn rut. This is the power of inertia. We are unable to integrate new information into our lives and make choices that allow us to grow. This is one of the most limiting, destructive forces I know of.

Adopting a posture of lifelong learning means you choose to seek out new information, to regularly push the envelope of your experience, to take appropriate risks, and to consider new possibilities. It is this very posture that will keep you from developing well worn ruts in your life.

John illustrates perfectly the principle of lifelong learning. When I first met John, he was an associate pastor of a growing, thriving church. He saw the fulfillment of his personal purpose in the pastoring, mentoring, and counseling of others. In fact, he thought he would one day be a senior pastor of his own church.

As I got to know John better, I discovered that what he enjoyed most about his job was conducting training sessions, speaking in public, and helping groups of people work through conflict. In particular, he specialized in helping other churches' pastoral teams resolve internal conflicts due largely to personality clashes and misunderstandings. And he was very good at it.

Ultimately, John was offered the opportunity to work as a self-employed trainer and consultant in alliance with a firm that served government entities, educational institutions, and small businesses of all types. The firm approached John after seeing his fine work conducting training and conflict-resolution sessions. Needless to say, this was a tough choice for John. He had a clear sense of his purpose, and he believed that the pastorate was an excellent way to fulfill that purpose. The power of inertia was strong. Being self-employed would mean giving up the sure paycheck. More importantly, could a consulting position really be a more appropriate venue for fulfilling his lifevision? Should he forsake the path of familiarity and proven effectiveness to take a risk?

After much personal soul-searching and discussion with close friends, John made the choice to leave the pastorate to become a full-time, self-employed business consultant. Though it had been an agonizing choice, he knew that a consulting career offered him an opportunity to work with a larger, more diverse group of people than ever before, while still fulfilling his life purpose. Yes, it meant a fair risk for John and his family, but he was convinced that the potential payoff in greater fulfillment and more opportunity to impact others was worth it. Would he have made the change without an attitude of being a "lifelong learner?" I don't think so.

I spoke with John recently, and he reflected on his past two years in the consulting business. John told me that he has learned more in the last two years than he did in the many years before his career change. There was something about going out on the proverbial limb, and then proceeding to cut the branch off, that catalyzed many learning opportunities for John. His first year was filled with many obstacles, not the least of which was a significant drop in his income. He kept at it, however, convinced by small successes that consulting was indeed the fulfillment of his lifevision. Year two has been much better. John has had some great client successes and nearly tripled his first year-income. It was fun to hear the good report, but it's what I expected of John all along. Lifelong learning is what he's all about.

Being persistent in learning

If at first you don't succeed, try, try again. We're all familiar with this simple saying. How often does it prove to be true in our lives? I can think of many situations where my first, second, or third attempt at something was less than successful. There is a lesson for us in each unsuccessful attempt: learning doesn't come easy, particularly when it comes to learning how to align your lifevision with your company's. Initial attempts at alignment can be frustrating, but I encourage you to persist. It's all part of the learning process. As Vince Lombardi said, "It's not whether you get knocked down. It's whether you get back up again." If you can see the possibility of alignment in the long run, remain focused on that goal and confident about your ability to achieve it.

When Tom and Emi decided to get married, they also decided to extend their partnership into the business world. Their desire to build a family business was part of their personal purpose, so they formed their own costume jewelry company. Emi designed sterling silver pieces; Tom found financing and subcontractors, and managed the books. Unfortunately, neither of them had much experience in the field. Their designs received praise, yet failed to find an instant home in the marketplace. Tom and Emi had no reputation or distribution network, and they quickly learned that these cornerstones of successful enterprise would take years of hard work to establish. Before long, they had to take full-time jobs to pay the rent.

Instead of giving up, Tom and Emi rededicated themselves to their long-term goals. Within a few years they were able to expand their product line, build a national distribution network, and establish a strong reputation among retailers. Their products have been featured in national trade magazines and won several awards. Tom and Emi still have to take on outside work, but they expect their jewelry company to be totally self-sufficient within another year or two. Their persistence will allow them to make their work an essential part of their lifevision.

The role of failure in learning

Life holds plenty of opportunities for trial and error. That makes it exciting on one hand and very frustrating on the other. No matter how educated, skilled, or experienced we are, there will always be moments of failure in our lives. In fact, some of the most brilliant, successful people have had more than their share of failure. It's not the amount or frequency of failure that is important, but how we respond to moments of failure.

Just as a sharp pain in our body is a signal to the brain that something is not quite right in a certain area, moments of failure often carry messages for us. Something went wrong. Why? Was it something we did? Was it the result of a blind spot we have? Did we misinterpret the information or screw up the communication process? Were we unprepared? Did we use the wrong methods or tools? As we sift through these types of questions, we'll have an opportunity to learn from our failure. Maybe the situation was entirely out of our control and completely due to external forces, but it's more than likely that we contributed to the failure in some way. Therein lies the opportunity to learn and to make a change for the better.

The real tragedy of failure is that we treat it much like the child touching the hot stove. The consequences are often severe enough that we don't want to risk failure again. When presented with a choice, we take the safe road. We may stop taking risks altogether, or settle for far less than we are really capable of achieving. The physical, mental, or emotional pain of past failure overtakes the possible benefit of trying again. And that is very unfortunate.

Last year I encountered a pretty painful consulting failure. I had been asked to design a change management process for a West Coast firm that had been a client of mine for about a year. I enjoyed the respect of the company's chief executive, and the company was a growing, exciting organization with which to work. Everything seemed to indicate that the consulting project would be a success. Together with the client, I designed a year-long process of workshops that would help employees understand the changes we were trying to implement. I brought in a colleague of mine to assist with a couple of the workshops. He did a great job, and the client ended up really taking a liking to my colleague. They began to question my process and if I should be the one to lead them on the change journey. One thing led to the next, and soon I was on the outs. My colleague was hired to finish the process.

In fifteen years of consulting with organizations, I had never had something like this happen. Though the client said he wasn't rejecting me so much as embracing my colleague, that's not the way I saw it. I had failed. As I realized this, I knew I had a choice. I could either use this failure to learn something, or I could let it get the best of me. As I reflected on the project, I began to see where I had made some improper assumptions. In short, I had presumed upon my great relationship with this client and hadn't delivered what the firm really needed. I had to confront my own role in the failure and use this experience to help me on the next client engagement. I was determined to learn from it and get on with life!

Too many people stop short of fulfilling their lifevision because they're stuck. They're allowing some past failure to get the best of them. I've met many such people over the last fifteen years. Though their circumstances vary, they're all in similar spots. Sadly, they've surrendered their dreams and aspirations and are settling for something less.

Reflect on your past failures for a minute. How have you dealt with them? Have you learned from them and gone on? Have you continued to repeat the same mistakes? Have you decided that the pain was too great, and opted out of trying again? Are you stuck in your lifevision journey because you can't let go of your past mistakes?

Accept responsibility for change

Discovering, aligning and renewing your life purpose is your responsibility. Although you'll need the help and input of others, you're the only person whose actions and attitudes you can control. You must choose to discover your lifevision and align it with your company's purpose. As I shared in Chapter 5, don't just wait for your company to align with you.

Maybe you're particularly unhappy about your current state of affairs or about a series of events that happened to you in the past. Maybe you're living with regret about a past opportunity you missed. Perhaps you've been burned by coworkers, an ex-boss, or even family members. Maybe you've accepted the pro-nouncements that others have made over your life: "you'll never be able to...," "you'll always be a person that...", "if you were like so and so..." I want you to know that it's not too late to change or to break the dysfunction in your life. You can accept the personal responsibility to make a change. You can overcome the past. You can write a new chapter for your life.

I once consulted with an individual who had a fair amount of dysfunction in her past. This middle management level person (I'll call her Karen) wasn't going anywhere with her company. She was an average, but acceptable, performer. The company didn't seem to mind, as long as Karen did her job to its minimum standards. Yet Karen was frustrated and unhappy. As we talked one afternoon, Karen revealed that she had always thought of herself as an average person with average abilities. She felt that she would never be really successful. The conversation took a deeper turn. We explored Karen's past and discovered that her failures had become reinforcement for her "average thinking." Her parents reinforced the label of "average" by saying that her failures demonstrated that she would never amount to much.

As I exposed her erroneous thinking about past failures, some glimmers of light seemed to be breaking through for Karen. It was a touching thing to watch. It was really just the beginning of her journey into discovering and fulfilling her life purpose. I have had the privilege to watch Karen grow and change since that profound moment over three years ago. Karen is now a division head of an exciting company and has become an accomplished public speaker. She has shed the average label and her past failures. She turned them into an opportunity to change and grow. She is living out her special lifevision with gusto.

Rising Above Mediocrity

Early in my career, my brother-in-law Hap told me about a profound truth he had discovered: many people are satisfied with mediocrity. As a business consultant, I have observed the motivations and behaviors of thousands of people in middle-market companies. I have concluded that Hap was right then and still is today. While a few people in every organization exhibit a commitment to excellence and demonstrate that they are not satisfied with the status quo, many seem content to "put off until tomorrow that which could be done today." This type of attitude results in a lot of "averageness" in the workplace. I would further characterize this phenomenon of averageness as a sort of whirlpool. It seems to gain momentum and critical mass, sucking people from the fringes into its vortex. Once in its grip, you become comfortable and satisfied with the present, and downright resistant to continuous improvement and change.

Your challenge and your opportunity, quite frankly, is to rise above this tide of mediocrity. The key to rising above it is a commitment to discovering, aligning, and continuously renewing your lifevision. In overcoming the tendency toward averageness, there are few other things that will give you more leverage.

An active commitment to discovering a unique lifevision brings an energy and vitality unlike any other I've experienced. I've observed this awakening in many others. Once you believe that there is a special purpose for your life, a transformation of sorts begins to happen. You see the world in a different light. You become more energized and passionate about your lifevision. It is one of the most profound and exciting events that can happen to a human being.

Each of us was created with an inner desire to join with something bigger than ourselves. We want to be part of a community or a collection of communities. We find real satisfaction in connecting with others in meaningful contexts like work, church, and family. From this perspective, the process of aligning your lifevision with your work makes profound sense. Since work is the one community in which you spend the greatest percent of your waking hours, why shouldn't you be actively aligning yourself with the bigger purpose of the work organization that you belong to? As you do, both work and life in general take on new meaning.

Overcoming the malady of averageness involves a commitment to renew our lifevision. Renewal, by definition, brings new life, new energy, and new perspective. Taking the time to renew and then to apply regained energy can be a difficult job. We are often consumed with the day-to-day, the beckoning of the urgent. The need to renew and the difficulty of creating the space to do it creates a healthy tension in us. If we respond appropriately to that tension, we can overcome the tendency toward mediocrity.

Jack's story helps to illustrate my point. Jack is the managing partner of a small professional services firm in Portland, Oregon. When I first met Jack a couple of years ago, I was quite intrigued by his set of circumstances. For most of his life, Jack had been a high performance individual, committed to excellence in himself and in helping those around him. At the time we met, Jack was struggling with a period of accepting mediocrity in himself and his firm. He had hit a point that many of us have encountered on our life's journey. The difficulties of the present had beaten him down to the point of accepting and somewhat embracing mediocrity as a way of life.

As we built a relationship over the next few months, I challenged Jack to discover his personal purpose and to more clearly define his firm's purpose. I challenged him to personally align his lifevision with his company's and to create an atmosphere where his employees could also align. I challenged him to commit to a process of renewing his lifevision and that of his firm's.

I recently spent a couple of days with Jack's management team, and it's exciting to see what has happened in two years. Jack is passionate and energized about his purpose and his firm's. His management team is experiencing a new dynamic in the workplace. They've put together a monthly newsletter full of the heartfelt expressions of several employees. One person is clipping out inspiring quotations and passing them around. Jack shared with me the work they had done on defining their mission, vision, and values by proudly showing me a laminated card articulating these elements. I happened to see the card on several other desks. The firm is receiving new business at a healthy pace, and people are taking responsibility for really making it happen. Together, they are overcoming mediocrity. They are rising above averageness. They are becoming a high performance organization. And that's very exciting!

Reinventing your lifevision

Arthur Schopenhauer said, "Our life is like a journey on which, as we advance, the landscape takes on a different view from that which it presented at first, and changes again, as we come nearer." So it is with your lifevision. As you advance on the journey, you gain new perspective. The change in your life circumstances brings new enlightenment which may result in shifts and changes in your lifevision. As you encounter change and challenges in your life, it's important to ask yourself if it's time to reinvent or significantly alter your lifevision. Although it won't happen very often, you will probably reach a few junctures in your life where the appropriate response is the re-creation of your lifevision.

Clara Barton, founder of the American Red Cross, was a woman with an incredible sense of purpose, centered around the concepts of giving and helping. The practical outworking of Clara Barton's purpose had at least three distinct expressions. She was initially well known for her service on the battlefields of the American Civil War, earning the moniker "Angel of the Battlefield." Her selfless giving in managing the dispensation of medical supplies and food during treacherous circumstances made her a household name in military circles.

Her efforts did not end with the war. She went on to form one of the first government agencies of the United States, directing a far-reaching effort to locate missing persons and reunite them with family members. Finally, we know her as the founder of the American Red Cross. For twenty-six years Clara Barton led the American Red Cross, setting a powerful example by personally leading multiple relief expeditions. She greatly expanded the traditional battlefield mission of the International Red Cross by involving the American organization in numerous peace-time disaster relief efforts. Here was a person with a clear sense of destiny, ministering visibly in the public arena. Her life was committed to giving, yet her purpose was not confined to a singular expression of service. Rather, she adapted with the changing times and changing needs of society. She successfully fulfilled her purpose to serve humanity by creatively reinventing her life-vision with the changing times.

Life will present each of us various stages on which to act out our unique destiny. We may not always be with the same company or live our entire lives in a particular geographic area. We need to remain open to the morphing and adapting of our lifevision.

While its central tenets may not change, the practical working of it most likely will.

This creates a challenging tension. How do we know when it is time to make a major change and reinvent our purpose, to make a break with the past, to take a risk and embrace the future in a new way? When do we embark on a new expression of our purpose by doing something different? There are no easy answers to these questions. Such changes should not take place without serious thought and contemplation. We would be wise to receive the counsel of others that we love and respect in order to fully examine all of the alignment issues. Ultimately, it comes down to faith. When you are convinced that it is time to express your purpose in a new way, you must take the leap and go for it.

Concluding thoughts on managing obstacles and change

Obstacles and change will always be part of your life. Instead of bemoaning this reality, determine to see your challenges as friends of your lifevision. I know it's a little peculiar to think this way, but it may just be the secret to fulfilling your destiny. Take George Washington Carver, for instance. We know him as the world-renowned scientist who discovered more than 300 marketable products using the lowly peanut and over 100 commercial uses for the sweet potato. Historians consider Carver the most influential person in the rejuvenation of the economy of the South.

What you may not know is that Carver was born a slave and was permanently separated from his parents as a little baby. In his driving quest for a formal education, he was refused elementary instruction by a white teacher. He pressed on and found a way to earn his high school diploma. Upon acceptance at college, he was again refused instruction because he was African-American. Overcoming this heartbreaking setback, Carver ultimately earned a master's degree in botany. He went on to become one of the most instrumental scientists and educators America has ever known. Talk about lifevision!

With his indomitable spirit and unrelenting pursuit of a powerful lifevision, Carver repeatedly overcame the obstacles and challenges in his path. He had several opportunities to be derailed. In fact, many of us would have cried "foul" and given up. But he persisted, embracing adversity and being strengthened by it. What a great inspiration for the rest of us.

Chapter 7 Tool Kit

Exercise 7-1: *Dealing with Change in the Past*

Reflecting on times of change can be a great learning tool. Think of a time of significant change in your past and how you got through it. Use the following list to jog your memory:

- Death of a loved one
- Going off to college
- Moving away from home
- Getting married
- Having children
- Going through a divorce
- Getting a new job

1. What do you recall about this time of change?

2. What emotions were you feeling? How did you deal with them?

3. What really helped you get through the change? What actions did you take that made the difference?

4. What does this past experience with change tell you about your ability to handle future changes? Are you encouraged that you can indeed handle change?

Exercise 7-2: *Overcoming Past Dysfunction*

This chapter included a discussion of overcoming dysfunction or negative events from your past. These might include:

- Tragic or traumatic events
- Major mistakes or errors you made
- Major opportunities you squandered
- Decisions you regret
- A breach of an important relationship
- Abusive relationships or family situations
- Illegal or immoral actions
- Being taken advantage of

1. Select one or two of these (or your own) and write a short paragraph or two about the event and the impact it had on you at the time.

2. Reflect on how your present behavior, actions and thoughts are affected.

3. Do you think it's possible to overcome the effects you've lived with? Why or why not?

4. Is there an action step you can now take to mend the effect of the past?

Chapter 8

Tapping the Power of Renewal

"The essence of living, really living, is renewal."
—Robert Waterman

The journey of discovering and aligning your lifevision may take you a lifetime. Most of us will spend our entire life in the discovery and alignment process. For me, this is what makes living such an excellent adventure. I've shared a lot of stories in this book, many of them about overcoming problems, pressing through difficulties, and learning from past failures. We all know that life is not easy. So how do we keep our resolve to move forward? How do keep on keeping on? To these questions there is a simple answer, although its application is not: renewal.

Human beings are wired to require rejuvenation. We can't sustain day-to-day activity without getting ample sleep. We can't go too long without a meal to recharge our batteries. We need weekend time to relax so that we're sharp and focused in our work. In short, we need to constantly renew ourselves or we'll burn out. Quickly.

Staying the course of fulfilling your lifevision can be a challenging endeavor. This is particularly true when things are not progressing as fast as you would like, or multiple trouble spots pop up at once. It is especially hard to fulfill your lifevision and remain a person of principle in the midst of difficult circumstances. Often the right choices for the long term don't appear to give you much payback in the short term. The temptation is to seek short-term relief, sometimes at the expense of lasting results. That is why renewal is so important. Day in and day out, you must commit to a process of personal renewal that gives you the strength, the insight, and the passion to keep moving forward.

Lifevision Diagram 8: *Renewal*

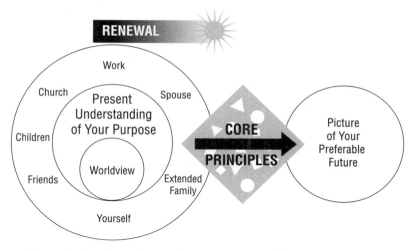

Principle: *Sustain and nurture your lifevision through renewal.*

Paradox: *The main source of renewal is outside of ourselves.*

In Chapter 7, I added obstacles to the progressive lifevision diagram. In Chapter 8, I am adding the key to overcoming the obstacles on a consistent day-to-day basis: renewal. While some people will choose to navigate life's obstacle course on their own, the majority of us need to tap into a fuel source to sustain our forward progress. The intentional act of renewal is the mechanism for you to tap the Energy Source.

You can make the choice to sustain and nourish your lifevision through the process of renewal, or you can choose not to. If you elect not to renew yourself, the opportunity to achieve your lifevision will be diminished. Life will become more of a crap shoot, and you'll be betting against the odds that you'll arrive at your planned destination. Through the process of renewal, you can push through even the most difficult circumstances, always making headway toward your preferable future.

Choosing to renew, however, is only the beginning of the renewal process. The challenge is in setting aside the time to renew and then making it happen. The paradox of renewal is this: the ultimate Source of renewal energy is not within you! While some postmodern spiritual gurus encourage you to look "within yourself" to tap the power, I encourage you to do the opposite. When the obstacles become large boulders standing in your path, the necessity of strengthening your faith and your resolve depends on your ability to tap into God's power. I have found this Otherworldly Power to be the most important element of my ability to sustain forward progress toward the picture of my preferable future.

In this chapter, I'll explore renewal from various perspectives. Specifically, I'll examine what renewal is all about, why you should choose to renew, and how you can take practical steps toward making it happen.

What is Renewal?

The definition that makes the most practical sense to me is:

The consistent, active process of connecting to the Creator so that you are empowered to:
- *discover, align and fulfill your unique personal purpose*

- *balance, integrate and grow in each of your lifevision communities*
- *become a person of principle*

Renewal is the process that facilitates the achievement of your lifevision. There are a few key points that help make this definition more practical:

- Renewal is, at its most basic level, a spiritual concept.
- Renewal, like water, restores life to your spirit.
- Renewal always involves the blending of the old and the new.
- Renewal always involves putting some things to death, while others come to life.

Renewal is, at its most basic level, a spiritual concept

In Chapter 2 I talked about the lifevision community of You and Yourself. As you will recall, this is the community of mind, emotions, body, and spirit. It is also the community where the process of renewal most actively takes place. If you accept the fact that you have the dimensions of mind, emotions, body, and spirit, then it makes sense that one of those dimensions is the center or focal point of who you really are. I believe that at your center you are a spiritual being. In essence, renewal is about reviving and revitalizing your spirit through connecting to the Creator, the ultimate source of spiritual energy and life. If you are indeed a spirit at the center, then you must nourish your spirit, guard it, and allow it to bloom. That is why renewal is the key to fulfilling your lifevision.

Just because your spirit is at the center of who you are doesn't mean the other dimensions should be ignored. On the contrary, the mind, emotions, body, and spirit are all connected. As such, active pursuit of mental, emotional, and physical health and growth are also important factors in maintaining your overall well-being. The process of personal renewal involves caring for each of your personal dimensions.

Renewal, like water, restores life to your spirit

Water is one of the most basic energy sources and is one of the core elements needed to sustain our human existence. Look at the natural landscape around you. Where there is water, there is life. Renewal, like water, brings life and refreshes us.

A poignant story that illustrates the centrality of water to sustaining life is the settling of San Diego. The Mission San Diego, founded by Father Junipero Serra, was the first European settlement of the San Diego area. Early letters document the frustration that the mission settlers encountered with the arid climate of San Diego. Multiple crop failures were the result of the unpredictable cycle of precipitation and the annual rainfall of roughly ten inches. The very existence of the San Diego mission was threatened by the lack of a dependable source of water to irrigate the crops. One of the letters from the Spanish government in Mexico City to the mission padres encouraged them to work through their obstacles. That is precisely what the mission fathers did. They developed a sophisticated flume system to carry water from the San Diego River in the Mission Gorge area over five miles from the mission. This was a considerable engineering feat, taking into account that it was 1816 and was accomplished without any modern technology. The San Diego mission not only survived but thrived with this new water source. San Diego has become a fine city as millions of visitors and residents alike can attest!

Like this story, your very life is threatened without access to water — the water of renewal. You cannot afford to be haphazard about your approach to renewal, waiting for the rain to fall in order to provide the necessary water. You need to be deliberate about building your water flume — your access mechanism — to ensure that you're tapping into the power of renewal. You need to actively plan to renew yourself and then take steps to fulfill that plan.

Renewal always involves the blending of the old and the new

Renewal encourages you to affirm the best of the past while you reach out to embrace your future. It does not mean you merely dispense with the old and grab on to the new. You must wisely preserve the precious foundations of your past while you seek to grow and experience the newness of tomorrow.

The process of renewal often brings something "old" into the forefront of your consciousness. Perhaps you may revisit something from your past experience which has become obscure through the passing of time. In my time of quiet reflection, I am often reminded of a childhood experience. As I think through the experience and attempt to discover how it has changed me, I find new insight for the present.

As you examine your past, I encourage you to identify your core competencies and talents, those things which you want to preserve and enhance in the future. What are the things you want to use as the foundation for your future growth? What about the core values and beliefs that have made you successful in past endeavors? The goal of the renewal process is to use these values as foundation stones. What about past relationships that have been especially meaningful to you? These are the relationships you want to strengthen or replicate with others as you move into the future. In short, embracing the best of your past provides a strong, stable foundation for the future fulfillment of your lifevision.

You must also identify aspects of the "new" that you want to add to your experience. Where are the gaps between your present reality and your vision of the future? What about the gaps between your current behavior and the external standards of truth and principle? These gaps will point to areas where you need to change and grow. The process of looking at your gaps will bring to light new truths or insights that you will want to incorporate into your life. For example, I have often discovered a "totally new" insight through scripture reading that has really helped me. As I have faced a challenge at work with a client or coworker, I have often found the encouragement I needed.

Another way to think of the blending of old and new is through the analogy of home renovation. Most home rehabs start out with an assessment of what is to be kept and enhanced, while considering the things you want to change or completely redo. A beautiful hardwood floor, a unique staircase, and a special alcove are examples of old features that you might want to restore and make prominent in the redone home. Similarly, the nonfunctional kitchen, the small bedrooms, and the narrow entryway are things you might want to totally redesign. Likewise, renewal is about enhancing your core competencies, talents and past experiences, while contemplating the new elements that you want to add to your life.

One of the interesting parallels between personal renewal and home renovation is that many people cannot afford to live somewhere else while their home is being renovated. They must endure the mess and interruption of remodeling while living in the house. When going through a personal renewal, you get the privilege of "living in the house while it's being remodeled." You get to try on the new while living in a state of change and transition. This is uncomfortable for most of us, but a necessary part of personal growth. Of course, most residential rehab efforts take twice as long as you think and end up costing twice as much, and so it is with personal renewal. It always seems to take longer than we want and to consume more effort than we would like!

Renewal always involves putting some things to death, while others come to life

While there are many things about my past that I want to preserve and build upon, there are just as many things that need to die. There's a proverb about seeds that goes like this: "Unless a seed is planted into the ground, it remains a solitary seed — basically useless. But if it is planted into the ground and 'dies', it bursts forth into abundant new life, yielding fruit that contains many new seeds."

We each have certain things — old habits, old ways of thinking, old memories, old behavior patterns — that need to die. They need to die so that new habits, new ways of thinking, and the like can begin to develop. These are the situations where the old cannot coexist with the new. The old must die off, and the new must replace the old. Renewal is the process whereby you make conscious choices to bury destructive habits or behaviors, outmoded ways of thinking, and the negative experiences of the past. In their place, with divine assistance, you can embrace a new way of living.

Why Renew?

Now that we have looked at what renewal is, let's take a deeper look at why renewal is so important. There are some key reasons why engaging in renewal is so necessary:

- Renewal helps you manage the seasons of change in your life
- Renewal helps to make the "familiar and routine" become fresh
- Renewal is the key mechanism for achieving your life-vision

Renewal helps you manage the seasons of change in your life

Life is lived in seasons. There are the primary seasons of infancy, childhood, adolescence, and adulthood. Within each of these there are secondary seasons tied into major life events such as going off to college, marriage, buying a home, the birth of children, the death of a loved one, divorce or separation, geographic relocation, career promotion or termination, and children leaving the nest. Each change of season brings a certain amount of stress and anxiety, regardless of whether or not the change is a positive one. For example, entering into a marriage is a wonderful event, but it can also produce a fair amount of stress and worry.

New seasons mean new stresses, new troubles, and new problems to solve. Renewal can be of tremendous help to you in the midst of all this change. In fact, because these events and circumstances are often those that you've never encountered before, the necessity of renewal becomes heightened. As the changes that accompany life's seasons threaten to overwhelm you, renewal restores you and gives you resolve to live through the circumstances. Renewal gives you present strength as well as future hope.

Renewal helps make the "familiar and routine" become fresh

Human beings are creatures of habit. Routines offer us security in the midst of increasing chaos and change. The rationale goes something like this: "Since there is so much change going on around me, I will control some of the simple things so that there is some amount of stability in my life."

But in the process of seeking stability, comfort, and security, have you fallen into a rut? A rut is really nothing more than a well-worn routine, one that becomes so well-practiced and familiar that it loses relevance. I'm not suggesting that you dispense with your morning routine of teeth brushing and showering — certain ruts are good! However, how many of your life routines or patterns have become stale? When is the last time you examined and challenged your TV viewing habits? Have you asked yourself recently if you are really doing the best you can to communicate with your spouse? How about your children? Are you in a routine, a rut of behavior with your kids, or are you challenging yourself to change the way you relate to them? Have you settled for mediocrity anywhere in your work? Have you stopped striving to achieve the best, just for the sake of some stability?

It's important to examine all of your life routines at least once a year. You should ask yourself which comfortable routines have become more of a rut. Once you answer the question honestly, you can use the renewal process to make positive changes for the future. The daily process of committing to something new in place of something old and familiar is one of the most important things we can do in establishing a new habit or practice.

Renewal is the key mechanism for achieving your lifevision

As you advance toward the fulfillment of your lifevision, you will certainly encounter the challenges and obstacles talked about in the last chapter. There will be many opportunities to be knocked off the path, to be sidelined with an injury. Renewal is the healing process that restores you, energizes you, and gives you the fuel to continue moving forward.

While there are many factors that come into play in the fulfillment of your lifevision, the personal choice to renew tops the list of things that can have an impact on your future. Much of life is out of your control. You cannot predict the triumphs and tragedies you will experience, but you can exercise your personal choice to renew and tap into the incredible power that is available. As you do, you will be propelled forward toward your lifevision.

How to renew: a daily process

I like to think of the "how" of renewal in two ways: the process of daily renewal and the occurrence of what I call "catalyzing renewal events" in your life.

In order to renew yourself, you must do more than mentally acknowledge the necessity of renewal. It's a common problem, especially in western culture; we mentally acknowledge something and believe that the acknowledgement is sufficient. In the meantime, our behavior doesn't change at all. You need to go beyond mental acknowledgment of renewal. Here are the practical elements of daily renewal that I have found most helpful:

Renewal of the Body — Regular exercise and good nutrition are the most important things for renewing your body. Particularly as you age, it is important to establish healthy habits to keep your body in good condition. Because your mind, emotions, spirit, and body are integrally linked, renewal of the body will yield benefits for your other personal arenas. Your mind will be clearer and your spirit more fresh.

Another seldom-practiced aspect of body renewal is the discipline of fasting. I have been practicing this discipline for about ten years. Although experts are just recently studying and learning more about fasting and its effects, I have found it to be a very powerful discipline. Perhaps the most noteworthy aspect about fasting is the increased self-awareness that results. Your most basic passions and emotions will be stirred as a result of denying your body its normal allotment of food. As the hunger pangs increase and the discomfort intensifies, you will get in touch with your most basic feelings and beliefs. If you use that experience to increase your self-awareness and make changes, to build on your strengths and compensate for your weaknesses, the discipline of fasting can yield big rewards.

Renewal of the Mind and Emotions — It seems that middle school is the time for project after project. Alyssa, my oldest daughter, has done everything from creating shadow boxes and science experiments to designing board games. You name it and she's done it. She recently asked me why I was headed to Portland for a few days. "I'm working on a client project up there, honey," I replied. "You mean that once I'm done with school, I'm still going to have to do projects?" It was one of those humorous, classic learning moments. Yes, life is a continuation of projects. We are always learning, always facing new challenges. Just as you need to regularly exercise your body, you need to keep exercising and challenging your mind. You need to assess the level at which you're being mentally challenged at work. Then you need to ask yourself what you can do to keep yourself mentally and emotionally sharp.

Some examples of things that can help you stimulate and challenge your mind and emotions are:
- reading books, periodicals, and newspapers
- visiting museums, nature centers, and the like
- engaging in deep conversation with an intimate friend
- visiting a park, preserve, or beach
- taking a vacation that incorporates a historical point of interest
- working puzzles or brain teasers

- listening to great music
- attending a theatrical production or concert
- continuing your education through a variety of venues
- developing a hobby or a skill outside your existing abilities

Different things work for different people. Establish some regular patterns of external stimulation using the activities that work for you.

Renewing the spirit: Ultimately, I think we need to "thank God" that it's Monday! The power, strength and light that you will receive from the Creator far outweighs even your best personal efforts at renewal. That is why I encourage you to develop an active spiritual life based on a personal relationship God. He is the ultimate source of renewal!

In order to establish a pattern of spiritual renewal in your life, it can be helpful to regularly set aside a time of quiet contemplation and reflection. During this time, you can choose among a variety of activities that will bring you refreshment:

- prayer
- Scripture reading
- meditation
- being totally quiet
- journalling

I use a combination of all of the above, and rarely use them in the same pattern. I prefer to be a bit more serendipitous about my spiritual reflection time. I don't really like recipes, so I freewheel it a bit, doing what seems right for that particular day. Again, the important thing is to commit to a regular period of spiritual reflection and renewal.

There is a classic mistake I see people making in their spiritual quiet time: they lack focus. Your spiritual renewal should always have a focus — to help you fulfill your personal purpose, enrich your interpersonal relationships, and help you become a person of principle. When I take time to spiritually renew, here are some questions I ask to help me focus:

- Where have I demonstrated unprincipled behavior lately? What were my motives in doing so? How can I find the grace and strength to change this behavior?
- Has my recent behavior been in alignment with and in support of my lifevision? If not, how can I move in that direction?
- Am I balancing, integrating, and growing in each of my interpersonal roles? If not, what adjustments should I make? Is each role contributing to my lifevision?
- What have I learned recently that might expand, clarify, or change my lifevision?

Honest answers to questions like these will give you plenty of food for thought. You'll know certain things you need to do, things you need to change, goals you need to set, time you need to set aside. It is in quiet reflection that I envision myself as I desire to be: fulfilled, purposeful, principle-centered, loving, growing. Do I ever achieve this ideal state? No. But I do believe that I have grown considerably in the last several years as I have actively pursued daily renewal.

How to renew: catalyzing renewal events

The daily renewal process is one that you must engage in diligently. It is a very deliberate process which yields powerful results. The other form of renewal is a combination of catalyzing events and your response to those events. Life's journey always includes certain energizing events that present you with an opportunity to make a quantum leap forward in fulfilling your lifevision. Perhaps the best way I can illustrate this is to share with you several examples of renewal events from my past:

- 1983: The Champaign Transition
- 1989: Finding My Place in Business
- 1992: A Renaissance Begins
- 1995: Westward Ho!

1983: The Champaign Transition

One of my most significant points of personal renewal occurred in 1983. I had just graduated college and was in the midst of several major life changes which I have collectively dubbed "The Champaign Transition." I moved to a new city, took a new job, joined a new church, and started a new relationship with the person who has been my wife of fourteen years. The natural event of graduating college resulted in a whole series of new things in my life. It was one of the most liberating seasons of my entire life. Through this time of opportunity, full of change and risk, I experienced an extended season of renewal. Tremendous personal growth was the result, the fruit of which I am still enjoying today.

1989: Finding My Place in Business

Another major renewal happened in 1989, when I struggled with the decision of leaving the consulting business to enter the ministry. It was at a church retreat for small group leaders that I experienced a profound energy and excitement around the idea of remaining in the consulting field as a "minister" of sorts to the business community. I knew that I could fulfill that lifelong calling to help others by remaining a business consultant and reinventing myself right where I was. This revelation catapulted me to a new level of consulting, and I experienced a time of personal vitality and energy. Years later, I picked up an article entitled "Minister of Commerce," about Tom Chappell, CEO of Tom's of Maine. The article talked about Tom's "call" to the ministry of business, essentially validating the choice I had made and giving me great encouragement.

1992: A Renaissance Begins

While facilitating a monthly roundtable of executives and entrepreneurs in 1992, I learned there was a real need for owners of small- and medium-sized businesses to have tools to guide their organizations through the tumult of the business environment. I made a personal decision to begin a search for practical methodologies that middle market companies could implement to become high performance organizations. This initial decision turned into an intense passion, marking a personal renaissance for me.

Over the last six years I have researched, developed, and tested practical tools for middle market companies to build and sustain high performance. I have called this collection of tools, borne of my own personal renewal, The Renaissance. It is interesting to see how leading an executive roundtable six years ago resulted in a profound season of renewal that has had an impact on me to this day.

1995: Westward Ho!

In late 1994, the opportunity to relocate to San Diego was presented to me by my firm. This seemed to be consistent with the firm's goals, but I wasn't sure about the opportunity lining up with my personal lifevision. This meant I needed to do a fair amount of personal contemplation and quiet reflection. It also involved a number of conversations with my lifevision communities. Through a deliberate process of weighing the offer in light of what I believed to be my life purpose, and with the counsel of a close circle of friends, my wife and I worked through this difficult decision. We decided a move to San Diego would be in alignment with our vision for the future, and in 1995 we were off to America's Finest City. This decision, of course, pushed us headlong into a season of change, growth, and renewal. New city, new office, new schools, new church, new everything. The natural circumstance of new surroundings stirred up a great season of renewal that has lasted for two-and-a-half years.

With each of the above situations, life gave me an opportunity to experience a season of renewal. In retrospect, the choices I made to participate in the renewal seem to be so obvious. Yet in each circumstance there was risk involved and a serious choice to be made. This will be common to the situations that you will face. Life will present each of you special opportunities for renewal, circumstances that may open the door to incredible personal growth as you make the choice to go for it.

Renewal and Faith

Life is an exciting journey. It takes us places we never thought possible. It challenges us with problems we never thought we'd face. As we reach out and touch others, their return touch has an impact on us. As we serve, we receive satisfaction and fulfillment. We grow and change. We mature and become more wise. All this happens through active times of doing, quiet moments of reflecting, joyous times of celebrating, and anxious periods of waiting. These are the things that characterize our journey and define our existence. Yet what gives real meaning to the tapestry of events and experiences is a knowing deep inside of us that we have a purpose to fulfill, a difference to make by being here. Something unique to do. Something special to accomplish.

You were created with a unique purpose to discover and fulfill. Postmodern thinkers may wag their heads at such a notion. They say that the universe is merely a collection of light, matter, and energy. Your life, like mine, is a random accident. We each move through our existence making the best of life, and then we die. I don't buy it. It doesn't add up. Its hollowness leaves me cold.

I've chosen to believe in an order and meaning to my existence. I've chosen to discover my unique gifts. I've chosen to reach out and serve a circle of people. I've chosen to make the world a better place for my having been here. These are the choices I've made in order to make sense of my life.

Believing in a personal purpose for my life does not make the discovery process, nor the fulfillment process, an easy one.

Ironically, it seems to make life more difficult in some respects. If I am not fulfilling what I believe to be my purpose, a certain sense of dissatisfaction and restlessness creeps in. It is in this place of tension, though, that our resolve is tested and strengthened.

What exactly gives me the reason to press forward? Why do I get back on the path after I've been blown off by a strong wind? Faith. A fervent belief in the uniqueness of my life and the importance of it in the grander scheme of human existence. A belief in Someone larger than myself coordinating a chorus of purposes and bringing them together. Although there is never enough evidence that I am fulfilling my ultimate lifevision, I grab onto simple milestones along the way that give me hope. It is the collection of these "hope milestones," married with a clear mental concept of the future and a persistent resolve to move forward, that form the essence of my faith. As I conclude this book, let me challenge and encourage you with the following poem.

Faith

Faith means that I reflect on my failures as learning experiences,

Faith means that I admit my inabilities to make it happen and yet keep going,

Faith means that I take a risk to push beyond the current limits of my experience,

Faith means that I am never satisfied with comfort and ease, but I'm always pressing,

Faith means that I see challenges as tests and opportunities to grow,

Faith means that I forgive wrongs done against me because grudges, revenge, and ill will sap my energy for moving forward,

Faith means that I reach out and join with others to make it happen,

Faith means that I celebrate the past, enjoy the moment, yet look with anticipation to the future,

Faith means that I will always feel the tension of the doing the old, while I wait for the new to come,

Faith means that I will press forward to fulfill my unique destiny, my lifevision, in relationship with the One who has created me to do it!

Chapter 8 Tool Kit

Exercise 8-1: *Mind, Emotions, Body, Spirit*

Most of us are familiar with various psychological models for understanding our human interactions. One that is widely known is the mind-emotions-body-spirit model of human dimensions. Take a moment to reflect on what each dimension means to you and what is important to you in that particular area. Now record your thoughts in the space provided.

Dimension	How am I doing right now in this dimension?	What would I like to accomplish in this dimension?	
		One year from now	Three years from now
Mind			
Emotions			
Body			
Spirit			

Exercise 8-2: *Renewal Events in the Past*

Reflect on a time in your life when you experienced a renewal event. Record your answers to the questions below.

1. Describe the circumstances that surrounded this event.

2. What is particularly memorable about that time in your life?

3. How long did your personal renewal last?

4. What did you do to sustain the renewal?

Exercise 8-3: *Renewal Events Now and in the Future*

After completing Exercise 8-2 concerning renewal events from your past, reflect on the following questions:

1. What renewal events are happening in your life right now, or could happen in the near future?

2. Where is the current or future renewal event most likely to be focused — spiritually, mentally, emotionally, or physically?

3. Is your behavior likely to be the same or different from the past renewal events that you've experienced?

4. What can you do to ensure that the current renewal is sustained or nurtured?

Appendix: Writing Your LifeVision

Results and Roses

The man who wants a garden fair,
Or small or very big,
With flowers growing here and there,
Must bend his back and dig.

The things are mighty few on earth
That wishes can attain.
Whate'er we want of any worth
We've got to work to gain.

It matters not what goal you seek
Its secret here reposes:
You've got to dig from week to week
To get Results or Roses.

Edgar Guest

When couples first marry, they often spend a lot of time dreaming about their future together. Often the talk centers on the subject of family. Generally speaking, young couples are filled with all sorts of ideas on how they are going to parent. They know quite well what things they will "never" or "always" do. However, when the first child is born, a couple moves quickly from the theoretical to the practical, and it is usually not without difficulty.

The same holds true in actually committing to print your first draft of a lifevision statement. It's one thing to think about it, meditate, reflect, and so forth; it's quite another to actually sit down with a pen or laptop and begin to write. Moving from the theoretical to the practical by actually writing something is difficult for many of us. There's something objective and measurable about the printed page. It launches you into the potential of accountability.

I strongly encourage you to give the writing process a try. Even though it may seem overwhelming or difficult, any attempt at drafting your lifevision statement is better than no attempt at all! Writing your lifevision may be easier if you take it one simple step at a time. That's how it happens for most of us.

Tips to Remember

Here are some tips to remember when writing your lifevision:

1. This process is interactive. We don't have the whole picture, and we need the input of others. Life was never intended to be a solo flight. Our lives are meant to touch others in meaningful ways, and vice versa. Our self-awareness will increase dramatically through the truthful sharing with others who are committed to us.

2. This process is evolving. Remember, this is just the first draft of many. As you grow and change, become more self-aware, experience pain, difficulty and loss, and weather different seasons of life, your lifevision statement will evolve. The closer we get to an object on the horizon, the more the landscape around us changes. Our perspective changes. Details become clearer. So it is with lifevision. Don't be intimidated by committing to print!

3. Each one of us is absolutely, totally unique. No two snowflakes are the same. No two mountain peaks or blades of grass are identical. Each one of us is wonderfully created, given a unique mix of personality and temperament, heritage, gifts, abilities, and passions. No two of us are identical!

Going Deep Enough

In his classic book, *why am i afraid to tell you who i am?*, John Powell aptly illustrates five levels of human communication. They range from Level One, cliché conversation: "How ya' doing?" or "What's new?", to Level Five, unedited self-disclosure: complete emotional, spiritual, and personal sharing of your deep heart. Just as Level Five conversations are healthy for our marriages and close friendships, perhaps we need "Level Five" thinking and sharing to make real progress in discovering our lifevision. Just as this level of disclosure is most difficult in many of our relationships, so this level of thinking requires the rawest kind of courage and hard work. The Tool Kit Worksheets found at the end of each chapter in this book require meditation, quiet reflection, prayer, solitude, and hard work, but the rewards are worth the risk!

Elements of a Good Lifevision Statement

It's been said that we really don't own something until we can write it down in our own words. There's a real germ of truth in that statement. Any written lifevision statement represents significant progress along the path of discovering purpose for our life. Over the years, my experience has taught me that there are certain identifiable elements that characterize effective, well-written lifevision statements:

- They reflect the three basic lifevision elements, PURPOSE, PEOPLE and PRINCIPLES. A lifevision that is missing one of these key ingredients may not be as powerful or meaningful over the long term.
- They transcend time, yet are contemporary and relevant. The unique destiny or purpose for our life is generally not constrained by time. Our purpose may not change much, although our particular strategy and tactics to fulfill our purpose may change, even with some regularity. The shape and form of the "current expression" of our timeless mission will be evolving.
- They sound like "you": Your goal should be to write a statement that fits you. It should reflect your particular strengths and uniquenesses. It should be written in language that is comfortable for you. Use language, expressions and written forms (poetry, prose, song, etc.) that are thoroughly you.

Starting Out Ain't Easy

Have you ever visited the origin of the Arkansas River high up in the Colorado Rockies? While the scenery is breathtakingly gorgeous, the headwaters of the river are rather unimpressive. You can hardly imagine that in a few hundred miles the little stream transforms into a raging mountain river, strong, powerful, full of life and beauty. The discovery and alignment of lifevision is the point of origin in unlocking the answers to the grander questions we all have about finding real meaning and fulfillment in our lives. The point of this book is to help facilitate the process, as small and unimpressive as it may first seem. My hope is that it acts as a guide on your journey of reflection, discussion, writing, thinking, adventure, and discovery — and that your life turns into a strong, powerful, joyful, beautiful river that touches hundreds of others in unique ways.

Summarizing Worksheets

In order to bring together the Tool Kit worksheets from the end of each chapter, this appendix includes two summarizing worksheets. These are both intended to assist you in drawing themes out of the Tool Kit worksheets you have completed. The process should look something like this:

1. Review the Tool Kit worksheets found at the end of each chapter.

2. Complete the Emerging Lifevision Themes worksheet at the end of the Appendix.

3. Complete the Purpose, People and Principles worksheet at the end of the Appendix.

4. Start a first draft of your lifevision statement.

5. Share your first draft of lifevision statement with five different people and gather their feedback for possible modifications. Consider a peer, a leader in your life, someone who views you as a leader, a spouse or significant other, and a person you know only from a distance.

Tool Kit Summarizing Exercise: *Emerging Lifevision Themes*

In reviewing each of your tool kit worksheets, use the "mind map" below to record some emerging themes. Each of the emerging themes can be placed in a "balloon." Balloons can be added and connected to the first circle of balloons, as additional details or thoughts come to you about a particular theme.

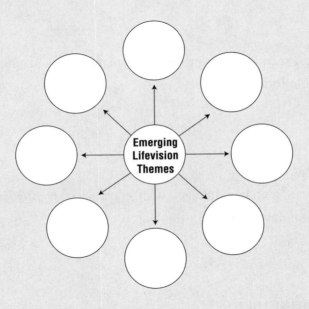

Tool Kit Summarizing Exercise: *Purpose, People, and Principles*

As you review your emerging themes and look over your other worksheets, answer these questions:

PURPOSE

Your understanding of your unique purpose is:

In executing your purpose, the picture of your preferable future looks like:

PEOPLE

You intend to interact with each of your lifevision communities in the following ways:

PRINCIPLES

You will bring your worldview into congruity with principles by:

Acknowledgements

The process of writing a book is certainly rewarding and meaningful. If the book is a success, the author receives a lot of accolades. What the reader doesn't see, of course, is the team of people that works in concert with the author to produce the final work. These people are vital to the successful end product. Their encouragement, their contributions, and their support really make the book what it is.

First, thank you, Toni, for your never-ending love, support and encouragement. When the times got tough, I knew I could count on you to keep me going. You've been a wonderful source of joy for fifteen years, and I look forward to spending the rest of my life with you!

Thank you Alyssa, Audra, and Kaley for keeping me sane and

helping me focus on what's really important in life! You are each a precious gift from God.

To Ben Hoerr: Thank you, brother, for your incredible contributions to this book. Thanks for your original material and thoughts, and for your honest editing and criticism. Thank you for helping me realize the Renaissance dream. Most of all, thanks for your love and support and telling me to go for it. You have inspired me in so many ways.

To John Chisholm: Thank you for participating in the brainstorm process that framed the content of the book. You're always good for that! Moreover, thanks for being my partner on this five-year Renaissance journey. You're a true friend and real encourager.

To Tony Moore: Thank you for your friendship and commitment. You have provided the leverage I so sorely needed to make the transition I did. I'm excited about being on the same team with you as we head into the future.

To Bob Harrington: Thanks for your friendship and loyalty. I appreciate your tenacity and gusto. I couldn't have done what I did without you. Here's to the future!

To Dianne Leman: Thanks for editing and offering your insights on the manuscript. Our discussions over the years have been a true inspiration for TGIM.

To Hap Leman: Thanks for helping me believe in my dreams.

To David Hodge: Thanks for being my business buddy for so many years. From the time we met through today, I have treasured our friendship. Thanks for taking a read of the book, and offering some very insightful feedback!

To Bill Jackson: Thanks for your leadership and friendship. The last year working together has been fulfilling and challenging, and I'm looking forward to the years ahead.

To Mike Martin: Thanks for taking the risk by investing in me. You are a true mentor and friend.

To Jack Talbot: Thanks for being one of my fans. It's always nice to know people are taking the message to heart and are making great progress. I appreciate your honest feedback on the book — you made me work that much harder!

To Don Williams: Thanks for welcoming Toni and me to San Diego. Your guidance as a fellow writer and speaker has been invaluable.

To John Shapiro: Thanks for your diligent efforts editing the book proposal — you opened my eyes to the world of writing and publishing!

To Dawson Church: Thanks, Dawson, for your insight and guidance in publishing this book. You've been a great help in spiriting the manuscript through all the paces.

To Mom and Dad: Thanks for being a powerful force in my life and shaping who I am today. Your shining examples are an inspiration to so many people. You truly walk the talk.

Most of all, thank you, Lord, for wisdom, insight, strength and the wind of your Spirit.

Bibliography

Baker, J.A. *The Business of Paradigms*. New York: William Morrrow and Company, Inc. 1992

Bennett, W. *The Book of Virtues: A Treasury of Great Moral Stories*. New York: Touchstone Books, 1996.

Block, P. *Stewardship: Choosing Service Over Self-interest*. San Francisco: Berrett-Koehler Publishers, 1993.

Chappell, T. *The Soul of a Business: Managing for Profit and the Common Good*. New York: Bantam Books, 1993.

Covey, S.R. *Principle-centered leadership*. New York: Simon & Schuster, 1990.

DePree, M. *Leadership is an Art*. New York: Dell Publishing, 1989.

Frankl, V. *Man's Search for Meaning*. Buccaneer Books, 1993.

Freiburg, K. *Nuts! Southwest Airlines Crazy Recipe for Business and Personal Success*. Bard Press, 1996.

Kanell, M.E. "Businesses are lulled by the job market: Reich." *Chicago Tribune*, December 28, 1997 (reprinted from The *Atlanta Journal and Constitution*).

Kidder, R. *Shared Values for a Troubled World*. San Francisco: Jossey-Bass Inc, 1994

Lancaster, H. "Stretching the Limits." *Chicago Tribune*, December 28, 1997 (reprinted from *The Wall Street Journal*).

Levering, R. and Moskowitz, M. "The 100 Best Companies to Work for in America." *Fortune*, January 12, 198.

Lieber, R. "Why Employees Love These Companies." *Fortune*, Jan 12, 1998

McGinnis, Alan Loy. *Bringing Out the Best In People*. Augsburg Publishing House, 1985.

Peck, S. *The Road Less Traveled*. New York: Touchstone Books, 1998.

Powell, J. *why am i afraid to tell you who i am?* Tabor Publishing, 1995.

Scott, R. *Scott's Last Expedition: The Journals.* Carroll & Graf, 1996.

Senge, P. *The Fifth Discipline.* Currency/Doubleday, 1994.

Steele, J. "Kinder, gentler image." *Chicago Tribune*, December 28, 1997.

Washington, B.T. *Up From Slavery.* Buccaneer Books, 1996.

Woodbridge, J. *More Than Conquerors: Portraits of Believers From All Walks of Life.* Moody Press, 1992